MW00639712

SAINT VINCENT SEMINARY FROM ITS ORIGINS TO THE PRESENT

DANIEL J. HEISEY

WITH A FOREWORD BY JEROME OETGEN

SAINT VINCENT ARCHABBEY PUBLICATIONS

2006

Library of Congress Cataloging-in-Publication Data

Heisey, Daniel J.
      Saint Vincent Seminary from its origins to the present / Daniel J.
      Heisey ; with a foreword by Jerome Oetgen.
            p. cm.
      Includes bibliographical references.
      ISBN 0-9773909-2-6
      1. Saint Vincent Seminary (Latrobe, Pa.)-- History. I. Title.

  BX915.L37H45 2006
  230.07'3274881--dc22

Printed in the United States of America
Saint Vincent Archabbey Publications
300 Fraser Purchase Road
Latrobe, Pennsylvania 15650-2690
http://www.stvincentstore.com

Cover photo: Bishop Connare ordaining deacons in the
Basilica, ca. 1963. Courtesy of Saint Vincent Archabbey Archives

Back cover: Ordination class of 1896 at the Cherry Path.
Courtesy of Saint Vincent Archabbey Archives

Book design by Kimberley A. Opatka-Metzgar
Editorial Assistants, Theresa Schwab, Joshua Whiteside and Sarah Yaple
Saint Vincent Archabbey Publications

To
Father David M. Hereshko,
Saint Vincent Seminary Ordination Class of 2000
Priest of the Diocese of Harrisburg

*The generous support of friends of Saint Vincent Seminary,
Mr. and Mrs. Edward A. Gromek and Mr. Jerome E. Lanzel, Jr.,
made possible the publication of this history.
The Seminary assures them of its continued gratitude and prayers.*

Contents

"The stranger who comes to the monastery, those with whom we share our riches, in our colleges and schools, should see us striving to be men of God, because we are men of faith and prayer."

Basil Cardinal Hume, O. S. B.
Remarks at Saint Vincent, 1980

Foreword

Institutional histories tend to be parochial and dull. This is especially true when they are no more than chronological recitals of one tedious episode after another, or when told not by a careful and critical observer but by a devout enthusiast whose purpose is to endorse and edify rather than teach and enlighten. So it is refreshing to read Daniel Heisey's history of Saint Vincent Seminary, a work neither parochial nor dull.

Rather it is an interesting and well-told story of one of the oldest Catholic seminaries in the United States, an important contribution to American Benedictine and American Catholic history.

Heisey juxtaposes his historical narrative with sketches of monks and diocesan priests who studied and taught in the seminary over its 160 years. These sketches personalize the narrative and engage the reader—everyone likes to hear about the people who make an institution live, which is why biography is such an enduring genre; and Heisey's judicious manner of selecting and inserting these mini-biographies contributes to the overall excellence of the work. He establishes the context of the seminary's history by providing cogent details from contemporary American, European, and Church history, and this also is fine, for it places the seminary within a broader perspective and "de-parochializes" the narrative, always a good thing in institutional histories.

Saint Vincent Seminary is a Benedictine institution, an apostolate of the oldest Benedictine monastery in the United States. Saint Benedict called his monastery a "school of the Lord's service." For him the Latin word for school, *schola*, signified not so much an institution as a gathering together of students and teachers for the sake of passing on a sacred inheritance. It is useful, I think, to see Saint Vincent Seminary as a school in this sense, something Heisey's work helps us do. The most important activity in such a school is not the transmission of information or even of knowledge from teacher to pupil —although the transmission of information and knowledge is certainly important —but rather the handing down from one generation to the next the wisdom of the Christian community.

Schools have been part of Benedictine monasteries from the beginning, and their chief purpose within the Benedictine tradition has always been to promote the growth of the Christian community in wisdom and grace. From sixth-century Italy the Benedictine heritage spread through the western world and planted deep roots. Monte Cassino, Jarrow, Whitby, York, Fleury, Fulda, Melk, Santa Guistina, Saint Germain des Prés, Eichstätt, Einsiedeln, Beuron, Maredsous, Downside, and Metten (to name just a few of the places through which the Benedictine heritage has been transmitted) constitute an historic continuum of which Saint Vincent, founded only in 1846, is a fairly recent addition. "We are dwarfs standing on the shoulders of giants," Bernard of Chartres said in the twelfth century. The giants on whose shoulders contemporary Benedictines stand include, in addition to Saint Benedict himself, such teachers as Benedict of Aniane, the Venerable Bede, Hilda of Whitby, Alcuin of York, Rabanus Maurus of Fulda, Abbo of Fleury, Ælfric of Eynsham, Hildegard of Bingen, Anselm of Bec, Ludovico Barbo, Johannes Trithemius, Augustine Baker, Jean Mabillon, Prosper Guéranger, Placidus and Maurus Wolter, Benedicta Riepp, and Boniface Wimmer. Strange names, yes, but giants by any measure, who give evidence of a very rich heritage.

The origins of the Pennsylvania Benedictines were in Bavaria, and for many years there was a strong German element in American Benedictine tradition. So in a discussion of Saint Vincent Seminary's history perhaps one will be forgiven for retelling a story from Germanic mythology. The story, much older than the venerable Benedictine Order, is about the pagan Teutonic gods Thor and Woden who roamed the forests of Bavaria long before Saint Boniface the Benedictine preached the Gospel there.

Thor, who gave his name to the fifth day of our week, Thor's Day, is usually remembered as the god of thunder. But he was also the god of order in Germanic mythology, responsible for defending the world, or Middle-earth as the early Germans called it, against the powers of darkness, the forces of chaos. It was said in the old days that every year Thor made a circle around Middle-earth, beating back the enemies of order. Thor grew older every year, and the circle occupied by the gods and men became smaller. It was then that the wisdom god, Woden, who gave his name to the fourth day of our week, Woden's Day, decided to intervene. Woden went out to the king of the trolls, who ruled over chaos. He got the king of the trolls in an armlock and demanded to know of him how order might triumph over chaos.

"Give me your left eye," the king of the trolls said to Woden, "and I will tell you the secret."

Without hesitation Woden gave him his left eye. "Now tell me," he said.

The troll said: "The secret is, Look with both eyes!"

The story reveals a great deal about the wisdom of the pagan gods —or the lack of it —and it goes a long way towards explaining why the Germanic gods did not survive. The only memory of

Thor and Woden that remains to us today lies buried in the days of our week. Is this story pertinent? Does it tell us anything about the Benedictines? To me at least it does. It is a story that reminds me of my Benedictine teachers. Not one of them would have given his left eye to the troll king.

I count myself fortunate to have been a student of the Benedictines for twelve years, four of them at Saint Vincent Seminary. The Benedictines who taught me in Georgia, North Carolina, and Pennsylvania were practical, fair-minded, knowledgeable men. They were intelligent and interesting, and what's more, they treated their students, inside and outside the classroom, as if we were intelligent and interesting too. As a student, I suspected this was one of the things they got wrong. But now I see that perhaps they got it right. Perhaps they saw more than we imagined. Perhaps in their wisdom and insight they saw us not as we were but as we would be—not as the acorn but the oak.

They were wise and insightful, these Benedictines. They looked at the world with both eyes. They were sensible and practical and down-to-earth, and most of them had a well-developed sense of humor, which came in handy when dealing with unripe acorns like us. Their manner of life was characterized by moderation, stability, hospitality to strangers, work, and prayer. What impressed me most about them, I suppose, was the way they spoke about God. Ethereal music did not begin to play mysteriously, nor did their voices turn solemn and eerie. Rather, when they spoke about God, they did so matter-of-factly. They might have been talking about Chuck Noll and the Pittsburgh Steelers. God was a reality they took for granted. Faith was what they lived every day. This impressed me when I was young.

It still does. Their faith was the kind that could move mountains —or perhaps, what is much harder, could move unripe students in the 1960s to think about God and eternity the same way we thought about football.

The Benedictines taught us the meaning of community: how a diverse mix of students and teachers and workers and guests could and should live together in faith and harmony with one another; how they could and should share both space and ideas, respecting each others' differences, making peace with one another after arguments and disagreements, celebrating together the good times, urging each other on through the difficult times, trying to keep up with those who forged ahead while giving a hand to those who lagged behind. They taught us that a true community of faith is always greater than the sum of its parts.

Our Benedictine teachers saw themselves as participating in a divine plan of which they and their community were an integral part. And most amazingly to us, they saw us, their students, as part of that community and part of that divine plan as well. It was clear to them, and they made it clear to us, that this plan was made manifest in history, in human history, and that this history was designed and executed by God, with some important help from us humans. It was a history that presumed a providential order in the world. But the providential order in the world was constantly being challenged and threatened by the powers of darkness, by pride and various forms of evil, by the forces of chaos, by the troll king. Our job was to pray and work and study hard so that we would know the truth when we encountered it, and so that we could distinguish that truth from the easy relativism and seductive falsehoods that run rampant in the world. Our job, in short, was to keep the faith, to look with both eyes.

In our materialistic, secular world, Benedictines continue to live a Christian, community life based on a first-century gospel and a sixth-century rule. They are future-oriented, modern people with roots planted deeply in a venerable tradition, an ancient wisdom. Saint Benedict taught that the true Christian devotes his life to seeking God. Fourteen centuries later the Benedictine author Jean Leclercq wrote that the Benedictine way is marked by a love of learning and a desire for God. Benedictine education embodies this Benedictine way and instills in those who open themselves to it a firm and practical faith, a deep respect for history and tradition, a sense of community, and a life-long commitment to hard work and frequent prayer. Daniel Heisey shows in his commendable work that the Benedictine tradition is alive and well at Saint Vincent Seminary.

Jerome Oetgen
April 21, 2006
Feast of Saint Anselm
Rome

Benediction in the Basilica, ca. 1958

Diocesan seminarians ca. 1958

PREFACE

Since its first days, Saint Vincent Seminary has sought to prepare priests to serve God in the Catholic Church. Within recent decades it has also taught religious sisters, members of the laity, men called to the permanent diaconate, and monks who are called to serve the Church as brothers. In all cases, the degrees offered have behind them "the Catholic faith that comes to us from the Apostles." What follows in these pages is a brief history of Saint Vincent Seminary, from its origins and its canonical establishment by Pope Pius IX to the present day. Local matters such as buildings and curriculum, as well as currents flowing from distant shores, draw our attention. In each chapter, while keeping an eye on the wider historical scene, I consider in particular the lives of at least two seminarians, one religious, the other diocesan, and with four exceptions, I avoid discussing at length anyone still living at the time of writing. This selective approach seemed best to prevent an unwiedly volume from emerging; past and present, though, men and women of interesting lives and inspiring character, all with many years wise service to the Seminary, made selection a challenge.

Scholars rely upon one another; as with the rest of life, "no man is an island." We owe perpetual debts to far more learned men and women who have gone before us. As Bernard of Chartres said in the twelfth century, we are like dwarves standing on the shoulders of giants in order to get a better view. Here I happily acknowledge my debt to Father Anselm Ober (1915-2000), a Benedictine of Saint Vincent. In 1938 he wrote a thesis for his bachelor's degree at Saint Vincent College, his subject being the history of Saint Vincent Seminary. Much of what we know about the first half of the Seminary's history we owe to Father (then Frater) Anselm.

Even more important to any study of Saint Vincent Seminary are the written works of Jerome Oetgen. An American diplomat, Dr. Oetgen has written numerous articles, mostly on monastic history, as well as a biography of Boniface Wimmer, *An American Abbot,* first published in 1976, and revised in 1997, and a history of Saint Vincent Archabbey, *Mission to America,* published in 2000. I am thankful not only for his learned works, but also for his kind conversation and wise insights.

A third source to acknowledge is Father Joel Rippinger, O. S. B., monk of Marmion Abbey. For one fascinating week in June, 2003, he gave me further understanding of monastic history in the United States. The occasion was the annual summer school for junior monks in North America, and a balmy stay at Saint Gregory's Abbey in Shawnee, Oklahoma, was enhanced by Father Joel's amusing and animated lectures. Just as his intellect enriched, so have his prayers sustained me.

To keep pedantry to a minimum, let me say here that quotations from the Bible come from the translation by Monsignor Ronald Knox (published between 1948 and 1953). Also, when quoting from the documents of the Second Vatican Council, I have used the translation compiled by Father Austin Flannery, O. P. (published in 1996). Papal writings of John Paul II are published by the United States Catholic Conference. Since these works—biblical, conciliar, and pontifical—are customarily referred to by chapters or sections, citing pages in translations that have appeared in various formats seems to be as unhelpful to the general reader as it would be tedious for the historian.

For guidance in writing this history, my thanks go to Rev. Kurt Belsole, O. S. B., rector of Saint Vincent Seminary from 2000 to 2006. Advice and information came also from Rev. Cyprian G. Constantine, O. S. B., academic dean of the seminary. Special help came from Rev. Brian D. Boosel, O. S. B., assistant archivist of Saint Vincent Archabbey and lecturer in Church History at Saint Vincent Seminary. Also assisting in the archabbey's archives was Brother Matthias Martinez, O. S. B. I am thankful for the generous memories of confreres, notably Rev. Demetrius R. Dumm, O.S.B., the late Rev. Joachim Fatora, O. S. B., Ven. Patrick Lacey, O. S. B., Rt. Rev. Paul Maher, O. S. B., Rev. Paulinus Selle, O. S. B., and Ven. Timothy Waid, O. S. B. Invaluable editorial work came from Kim Metzgar, Theresa Schwab, and Joshua Whiteside of Archabbey Publications, and insights from the corporate world came from Paul Whiteside, Director of Development for the Seminary. Lastly, I would be remiss were I not to acknowledge the encouragement of the Rt. Rev. Douglas R. Nowicki, O. S. B., archabbot of Saint Vincent Archabbey and chancellor of Saint Vincent Seminary.

Brother Bruno, O. S. B.
Saint Vincent Archabbey

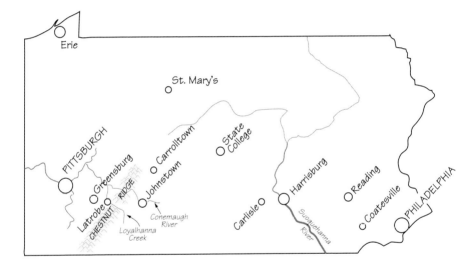

1

A CABIN IN THE ALLEGHENIES

Christianity is a religion of giving and receiving. God the Father gives His Son to the world; the Son returns to the Father with all those the Father has entrusted to Him; given among them all and binding them is the gift of the Holy Spirit. From all eternity, God the Father pours forth His love to His Son, who eternally receives that love and reciprocates it within the love of the Holy Spirit. Creation and salvation flow from this exchange of love among the Trinity. From the earliest days of the Church, Christ's followers have seen themselves as having been given a mission. "Go out all over the world," the risen Jesus told the disciples, "and preach the gospel to the whole of creation" (Mark 16:15).

In the sixth century of the Christian era, Saint Benedict of Nursia stipulated in chapter four of his Holy Rule that monks were to use the tools of good works within the monastic enclosure; the idea being that charity begins at home.[1] Saint Gregory the Great, in his life of Saint Benedict, makes clear, though, that the first monks under the yoke of the Rule also performed charitable works for the local laity.[2] One should not be surprised, for the roots of such a balance between prayer and good works lie in the Jewish tradition. "Do not lose confidence in thy praying," said one sage, "or leave almsgiving undone" (Sirach 7:9). The Benedictine Rule is known for this sort of unity of spirituality and practicality. "It shows the way to religious perfection," said one who had studied under the monks of Saint Vincent, "by the practice of self-conquest, mortification, humility, obedience, prayer, silence, and retirement from the world and the concerns of the world."[3]

In the midst of the many missionary ventures of the Church, significant to the origins of Saint Vincent Seminary is the mission that converted Germany, where, according to Tacitus, "good morals availed more than good laws elsewhere."[4] Saint Vincent was founded by German monks, their leader, Boniface Wimmer, receiving the monastic name of Boniface upon his entry into the monastery, a name that held deep significance for German Catholics. Saint Boniface was an English monk who in the eighth century brought the Gospel and the Benedictine Rule to the Rhineland, where he established monasteries and served as bishop of Fulda.

Saint Boniface in turn had been inspired by the life and writings of Saint Bede the Venerable, an English monk who rarely left his monastery in the north of England but who nevertheless influenced and encouraged missionary activity. Near the end of his life, Bede wrote to Egbert, the new bishop of York, England, a former student of Bede. Bede reminded the bishop of the importance for the faithful of the diocese, many new to the Church, to receive daily Communion and to practice *lectio divina,* the prayerful reading of Scripture. When Boniface set about to share the faith with the pagans of Germany, he wrote back home to England for his confreres to send him the works of Bede.[5]

BONIFACE WIMMER

This legacy was well-known to Boniface Wimmer (1809-1887), founder and first abbot (later archabbot) of the Benedictine monastery of Saint Vincent.[6] Sebastian Wimmer had been a priest of the Diocese of Regensburg, Bavaria, who had discerned a call to monastic life, and in the course of time he also discovered a calling to be a missionary. As an ordained monk, Wimmer belonged to the Benedictine abbey of Saint Michael, in Metten, Bavaria. It dated to the eighth cen-

Archabbot Boniface Wimmer, O.S.B.

tury, when it enjoyed the generous patronage of Charlemagne, who asked the monks to pray for him and his empire. By the nineteenth century and the revival of monastic life after the suppressions by Napoleon, the abbey at Metten was under the royal patronage of Ludwig I, King of Bavaria. Wimmer's dream of work in the foreign missions of America found support from King Ludwig.

Wimmer's tumultuous story has been ably told by Jerome Oetgen, but here let it suffice to say that as a young monk Wimmer learned of the spiritual isolation of German Catholics in Protestant America. In 1846, Wimmer and eighteen young candidates for monastic vows landed in New York and began the long trek to western Pennsylvania, where the bishop of Pittsburgh had invited them to serve; after a dismal first try at Carrolltown, they moved some forty miles west to a struggling rural parish, Sportsman's Hall. Established in 1790, it had known a series of pastors, including two Franciscans, one Dutch, the other German. In 1835 a small brick church had been built and dedicated to Saint Vincent de Paul. The rectory was a log cabin, 26 by 28 feet; the original chapel, also of log, was 40 by 26 feet. By the 1840s both were in disrepair.[7]

BENEDICTINES INVITED TO PITTSBURGH

The idea of Benedictine monks serving as missionaries in America was not new with Wimmer. In 1794, Bishop (later Archbishop) John Carroll, whose diocese, all of ten years old, consisted of the entire United States, asked English Benedictines to come to America.[8] Carroll wrote to Michael Pembridge, a Benedictine priest at the priory in Surrey, "nothing can be more pleasing to me than the prospect of having in my diocese a settlement of English Benedictines."[9] Carroll assured Pembridge of his "attachment and veneration" for the Benedictines, saying that "they will honour and extend religion." The history of the Benedictines as missionaries brightened Carroll's thoughts. "I never can forget," Carroll added, "that they were the apostles of England, Germany, & many other countries."

As for a home for the monks, Carroll had studied his map. "I am decidedly of the opinion," Carroll wrote, "that the neighbourhood of the town, called Pittsburgh, in Pennsylvania, about 300 hundred miles from this [city, Baltimore], would be the properest place for a settlement and school." The English Benedictines had returned to England from France to escape the persecution brought about by the French Revolution of 1789; they had gone to France in the late 1530s to flee the persecution of the Tudors. Carroll was aware that Benedictines, especially those who had been refugees, needed stability and security. "This situation is far remote from, & as secure, as London, from the Indians: there is a continual communication of trade and regular posts from that settlement to Balt[imor]e, Philad[elphi]a, & all the trading towns on the Atlantic." He was not asking the monks to huddle in the forest primeval and await being scalped.

As for the size of monastic community Carroll had in mind, he seems to have recalled that Saint Benedict had founded twelve monasteries of twelve monks each. Carroll suggested that "twelve Religious, including, at least, four good laborious lay Brothers, who would be exceedingly useful, as your great distress there would be for hirelings, and the laws of Pennsylvania admit not slaves."

One notices that from the first, the Benedictines in America were to have a school. Moreover, the English monks seemed to have been concerned about isolation, hence Carroll's assurances of Pittsburgh's communication with the cities of the eastern seaboard. Just as Saint Boniface wrote home to England for books by the Venerable Bede, Pembridge and his confreres would have needed to write home and elsewhere. As they spread their faith and their culture, monks had to keep in touch with their sources. Benedictines, however book-ish their reputation, are not by nature hermits, and when a bishop sought them for his diocese, it was with full knowledge of the Bene-dictine heritage of Christian humanism.

Carroll's dream for Benedictines to settle in Pittsburgh faded away. Dreams recur, though, and they can be shared by others. In many ways, the apostolic succession of the bishops of the Catholic Church ensures the handing down of memories as well as teachings. In 1808, the territory of Carroll's diocese had been reduced, bishops in Boston, New York, and Philadelphia lightening his burden. In 1826 Rome created more dioceses, including New Orleans and Saint Louis; in 1843, westward migration helped form the new dioceses of Chicago, Milwaukee, and Pittsburgh.

Pittsburgh's first bishop, Michael O'Connor, saw the good that

Benedictine monks could do for his diocese, but rather than turn

Bishop Michael O'Connor

to the Benedictines of England, he entertained the prospect of monks from Germany. Around this time an English friend of the Irish, John Henry Newman, was writing essays about the early Benedictines, and he summed up the romantic vision of the time. Newman wrote of the tenacious simplicity of the Benedictine missionaries of Germany. "Amid the deep pagan woods of Germany and round about," Newman wrote, "the English Benedictine plied his axe and drove his plough, planted his rude dwelling and raised his rustic altar upon the ruins of idolatry," thereby laying "the slow but sure foundations of the new civilization."[10]

Wimmer had been preceded in western Pennsylvania by another German priest, Peter Henry Lemke. Lemke (1795-1882), a former Lutheran minister, had in 1824 become a Catholic, and two years later he was ordained priest. He left Germany and went to Pennsylvania to serve the growing population of Catholics, especially in the western half of the Commonwealth. While helping the missionary labors of Demetrius Gallitzin, prince and priest, Lemke had founded in 1840 Carrolltown, named in tribute to the archbishop, and to this day it remains a small town in Cambria County, its population still heavily Catholic. Lemke had returned to Germany to persuade other priests to come to Carrolltown. In Germany, Lemke had met Wimmer, and later he wrote to Wimmer in terms strikingly similar to those used by Newman. "The people are longing," Lemke wrote Wimmer, "to see the sons of St. Benedict swinging axes in the

American forests as they did a thousand years ago in the German forests."[11] Not only did this image appeal to Wimmer's sense of history and of mission, it was also the spirit bishops such as Carroll and O'Connor wanted for their dioceses.

LOG CABIN PARISH

When Wimmer and his monks arrived at the parish of Saint Vincent, they found it in a gentle valley reminiscent of their homeland. A quarter century before their arrival, an officer of the United States Army had described the area. After noting the rises to the east, Major Stephen Long said, "Chestnut ridge [sic]…is somewhat more abrupt and precipitous than those before mentioned."[12] He reported that Chestnut Ridge "is divided transversely by the bed of the Loyalhanna, a rapid but beautiful stream, along which the turnpike is built."[13] Today the road is known as Route 30; the Loyalhanna, often good for trout, meanders north to join the Conemaugh River, the waters of which eventually join those of the Allegheny.

Modern travelers thus see the lay of the land much as had Long

St. Vincent College, Beatty, Pa.
St. Vincent's in 1831.

and his fellow soldiers. "Few spots in the wild and mountainous regions of the Alleghanies [sic]," Long wrote, "have a more grand and majestic scenery than this chasm."[14] As Long surveyed the rolling valley west of Chestnut Ridge, he recorded, "the landscape presenting a grateful variety of fields and forests is often beautiful, particularly when, from some elevation, the view overlooks a great extent of country," and when "the blue summits of the distant mountains are added to the perspective."[15] When Wimmer first inspected property on Chestnut Ridge, it stirred his historical imagination. "The land itself is wild and rough, but romantic," Wimmer wrote in 1851, adding, "I feel as if I am transferred into the time of Clairvaux or the Cistercians."[16] Thus the setting of Saint Vincent, evoking for Wimmer the twelfth century, and largely unchanged in two hundred years.

Within sight of these primeval hills Wimmer settled, building an abbey and farm, a mill and a brewery, a college and a seminary. Wimmer, student of history and German romantic, cultivated the ideal of a self-sufficient monastery in the wilds of a new land; always before him was the example of his namesake, Saint Boniface. Wimmer had desired that the first monastic recruits he assembled be new to their callings. With rare exceptions, he refused any man who had set foot inside one of the vast and ancient abbeys such as Metten, with its Baroque ornamentation, elegant liturgies, and well-stocked library and wine cellar. Wimmer knew that they would find nothing of the sort awaiting them in their new home, and he did not want disillusioned monks in the wilderness pining for the comforts of their own Egypt. In the mid-twentieth century, an English monk admired Wimmer's commitment to the Benedictine ideal, noting that Wimmer was "determined to take his stand on the holy Rule wherever possible," to the extent that he "was bent on forming his monastery on agricultural as well as on missionary lines."[17]

For the first few years the going was hard, and the whole project seemed on probation. Whatever his flaws, Wimmer was not plagued with self-doubt. "Of middle stature and robust exterior," wrote one who knew monks who knew him, "Wimmer was a man of a very practical mind and marked determination."[18] Of the eighteen men who came with Wimmer from Bavaria, four were students for the priesthood. As Anselm Ober put it, "St. Vincent began as one large household,"[19] the divisions between its various schools and residences being vague. In the rough and tumble of those first years, not only rooms and buildings served many purposes, but also personnel.[20] "At first Fr. Boniface was the only teacher," Ober records, and in the morning Wimmer "lectured on Dogma and Moral [theology]."[21] It is likely Wimmer used as his textbook for dogmatic (today called systematic) theology Alois Buchner's *Summa Theologiae Dogmaticae*. In the special collections of the Saint Vincent library is Wimmer's own copy of this work, bound in three volumes.[22] In 1847, Father Peter Lechner, a German Benedictine of the abbey of Scheyern, arrived at Saint Vincent with some twenty lay brothers, and until 1850 Lechner also taught theology.

FIRST RECTOR

By 1856 Wimmer's monks could offer education from elementary school to seminary.[23] Directing the seminary part of this school was a priest who had recently entered the monastery at Saint Vincent, Demetrius di Marogna.[24] Born Carlo di Marogna in 1802, he had spent his early years in Tuscany; in 1809 the

Rev. Demetrius di Marogna, O.S.B.

family moved to Bavaria. His family was of the nobility in the city of Verona, and Carlo di Marogna held the title of count. He studied theology in Mainz, where in 1826 he was ordained; for twenty-one years he served as a priest in the Diocese of Augsburg.

In 1847 he sailed for New Orleans, moved to Chicago, and eventually settled in Germantown in southern Illinois. There he ministered to German Catholic immigrants, even applying medical aid during an outbreak of cholera. In the midst of these wanderings, he felt a longing for something more stable. In 1852 he entered the novitiate at Saint Vincent, and Wimmer soon recognized di Marogna's maturity and administrative gifts. Wimmer assigned him, upon making vows, to serve as prior of the monastery, and in addition to teaching in the College, Demetrius di Marogna was also made the first rector of the fledgling seminary. In 1856 Wimmer sent him to found a priory in Minnesota.

Wimmer and di Marogna taught Catholic theology to men feeling called to the priesthood, and Wimmer and di Marogna, by their teaching, followed a path cut almost three hundred years before. The idea of a seminary for training priests dated to the sixteenth century, the brainchild of Reginald Pole, an English cardinal exiled by Henry VIII. In a nation noted for gardening, it is fitting that Pole thought in terms of a seed-bed in a nursery. The idea found favor with the Council of Trent (1545-1563), and the Fathers of that Council mandated seminary education for men aspiring to holy orders. A seminary promised to educate the mind and discipline the will. In 1564, the first Catholic seminary in what is now Germany, following the decrees of Trent, opened in Eichstätt, Bavaria.[25] By Wimmer's day, providing seminary formation was not just Church law, it had become common custom.

First Ordination

The founding of the Seminary can be dated to 1846, the year of the founding of Saint Vincent, and in 1847, Saint Vincent saw the first of its seminarians ordained. He was Karl (also called Charles) Geyerstanger, O. S. B., a monk of Saint Vincent, and he had something

of a head start. Born in 1820 in Salzburg, Austria, Johann Martin Geyerstanger had studied theology in Munich. In 1846 he had come with Boniface Wimmer to begin a Benedictine monastery in Pennsylvania, and although still in simple vows when ordained by Bishop O'Connor, Geyerstanger must have shown great promise. One gathers he was a learned as well as pious man, for in the special collections of Saint Vincent's library is a seventeenth-century book of saints, and inside the front cover is the signature, "P. Carolus Geÿerstanger, Ord.

Rev. Charles Geyerstanger, O.S.B.

Sancti Benedicti."[26] One is thus reminded that most of the missionary priests of that era were at least tri-lingual.

The surviving photograph of Geyerstanger shows a profoundly unhappy man, but not everyone photographs well. In a monastery dedicated to the missionary apostolate, ordained monks were bound to find themselves sent into parochial work. The lay faithful could understandably conclude that the natural habitat of a priest is a parish, thus blurring in the popular mind the nuances of a monastic calling. Geyerstanger spent much of his priestly ministry in various parishes, from St. Marys, in northern Pennsylvania, to Newark, New Jersey. Other assignments included parishes in such small Pennsylvania towns as Bellefonte, Carrolltown, and New Germany. Geyerstanger's years in parishes began a symbiotic cycle that one scholar has dubbed "the monastic circle of life."[27] Monk priests in parishes served as models and inspirations to young men who were discerning callings to monastic life, whether ordained or not, and so these young parishioners sought entry into the home monastery of their priest. Here was Wimmer's vision at work, pastoral, educational, and monastic apostolates weaving together to form one fabric. From 1864 to 1879, Geyerstanger was pastor of the parish at Saint Vincent, and from 1870 to 1874, he served the abbey as choirmaster. He died in 1881 and was buried in the abbey cemetery.

DAILY LIFE

In these first years of the Seminary, seminarians came from the monastic community and the Diocese of Pittsburgh. According to Anselm Ober, a typical day at Saint Vincent Seminary in the 1840s and 1850s followed a monastic horarium.[28] This schedule Wimmer adopted from that of Metten. At a quarter to four, the monks roused themselves from sleep, roughly six hours' worth, and by four they were in the church. There in the choir Wimmer led the clerics and the students in Matins and Lauds in Latin, while in the nave the lay brothers recited the Joyful Mysteries of the Rosary in German. An hour later there was "meditation," followed by breakfast and then conventual Mass. While the others were at breakfast, Wimmer stayed in the church and prayed the Office of Prime.

After Mass, the lay brothers went to their respective tasks, and the students went to school. At nine there was Terce and Sext; at quarter to eleven, all assembled again in the church for their daily examination of conscience. At eleven, the mid-day meal (whether one called it lunch or dinner) with table reading, followed by adoration of the Blessed Sacrament and then None. From noon to one there was community recreation, while the lay brothers returned to the church to recite the Sorrowful Mysteries.

In the afternoon was time for studying or classes, and Vespers was at three. At five Wimmer had a class for the monks on the Holy Rule, and at 5:30 there was time for spiritual reading. At six, the

Seminary regulations, in Latin, from the nineteenth century.

evening meal, called supper, lasting half an hour; as with the noon meal, there was table reading. After supper, another period of community recreation, after which all returned to the church. There, at 7:30, the lay brothers recited the Glorious Mysteries, while the others chanted Compline. By nine, all were in their respective rooms, and Grand Silence prevailed. At 3:45 the next morning the community gathered again for Matins and Lauds. Still, outside of prayer, silence was kept until after breakfast, a custom maintained at Saint Vincent into the early 1970s.

Canonical Foundation

Part of Wimmer's energies went to establishing the monastic identity of his community by securing its rights under canon law. He locked horns with Bishop O'Connor, who saw the monastery as part of his care. Wimmer knew that even in the eighth century, the monastery of the Venerable Bede had enjoyed independence from the local bishop. More immediate an example was the abbey at Metten, free from the bishop of Regensburg. Such autonomy was guaranteed by the pope; an exempt monastery stood under his jurisdiction. In 1853, Wimmer had been granted his request of the Holy See for Saint Vincent to enjoy the status of a priory, and he then set about petitioning Rome for conferral of the rank of an independent abbey, exempt from the control of the local bishop.

Bishop O'Connor objected to this petition, making the not unreasonable point that such a request was premature, given the recent elevation to the rank of priory. The bishop also had doubts about the fitness of the blunt and headstrong Wimmer to be an abbot. While insisting that he objected only to the timing of the petition, O'Connor added that the nascent seminary at Saint Vincent must admit diocesan students free of charge, and he stipulated that such students, over whose selection the Seminary would have no say, must make up at least half the student population. This demand would be seen as absurd by any school, and Wimmer flatly dismissed it.

Nevertheless, resistance from the local ordinary put a brake on the slowly grinding wheels of Vatican bureaucracy. Wimmer, seeing obstacles as opportunities, packed his bags and in December, 1854, set off for Rome. He stopped first in Bavaria, where he rallied his patrons and benefactors to his cause. Then, shades of Hannibal, he crossed the Alps and made south for Rome, where he arrived in April, 1855, in time for Holy Week.

In Rome, Wimmer stayed at the Benedictine monastery of Saint Paul's Outside the Walls and made the rounds meeting with members of the Curia, including Abbot Angelo Pescetelli, O. S. B. Pescetelli was procurator general of the Italian Cassinese Congregation of Benedictines, and he had been asked by the Vatican to serve as advocate for Saint Vincent in this case. Wimmer knew his own limitations as a salesman. "I speak plainly even in Latin," Wimmer wrote to King Ludwig, "but if I must defend right against wrong, I have a still franker language."[29] Pescetelli guided Wimmer and his file through the bureaucratic channels, which had circumstances been different, one could call Byzantine. All the while, Wimmer's personal diplomacy, however blunt at times, helped his cause. In June, 1855, Wimmer was granted a private audience with the pope.

One imagines seasoned veterans of Vatican *Realpolitik* such as Pescetelli and Pius IX smiling discretely as the ever direct Wimmer, his dream at stake, argued with fervor in Germanic Latin. In his audience with the pope, Wimmer was deferential yet firm. His sense of commitment, as well as his integrity, must have been evident to all. A monk in his position would not cross the ocean, leaving behind a fledgling monastic community, if he had been filled with lukewarmness.

Pope Pius IX

On 24 August, 1855, Pope Pius IX issued *Inter ceteras*, a papal bull raising Saint Vincent to the rank of an abbey, fully exempt from control by any bishop.[30] Wimmer was named the abbot of the monastery. The bull also gave canonical foundation for the College and the Seminary. It further allowed for the creation of a congregation of abbeys and priories founded by Saint Vincent. This monastic congregation became the American Cassinese Congregation of Benedictines. Wimmer returned to Saint Vincent triumphant, and once home, he and his monks chanted the *Te Deum* and celebrated Benediction.

WORLD EVENTS

Local history, even institutional history, can become myopic, so from time to time one does well to stand back and see what was occurring elsewhere. In 1855 Franz Liszt was composing his "symphonic poems" and entertaining and enriching audiences in his native Hungary and across Europe with his dynamic performance on the piano. Also in that year, a bureaucrat in the British postal service, Anthony Trollope, published his fourth novel, *The Warden*, thereby opening to generations of readers the amusing world of Barchester, a mythical cathedral town in the English countryside.

Of course, life was not all classical music and tales about the foibles of Anglican clergy. In eastern Europe, the "thin red line" of Queen Victoria's army fought the Russian forces in the Crimean peninsula. The Crimean War, or the Russian War as it was often called then, contained Russia and kept it from encroaching on "the sick man of Europe," the decrepit Ottoman Empire of Turkey. In 1854 the most memorable event of that war had occurred, the charge of the Light Brigade, in the planning of which, in Alfred, Lord Tennyson's precise yet understated words, "someone blundered."

Closer to Saint Vincent, in February, 1855, James Pollock, governor of Pennsylvania, signed the charter for the Farmer's High School, later known as Penn State University. More than a century later, in 1961, priests from Saint Vincent became the Catholic chaplains at Penn State. In March, 1855, in Pittsburgh, Andrew W. Mellon was born. In time he inherited the bank that has long borne his family name, and he distinguished himself as Secretary of the Treasury (1921-1932) and as the founder of the National Gallery of Art in Washington, D. C. Also in the mid-twentieth century, members of the Mellon family became well-known benefactors of Saint Vincent, especially its library.

EMMERAN BLIEMEL

Two seminarians from the 1850s deserve mention. One served the Church as a parish priest and then as a military chaplain; the other served as an abbot. In 1855, when *Inter ceteras* appeared, a year from ordination was a young monk born in Bavaria, Michael Bliemel.[31] In 1851, at age twenty, he had entered Saint Vincent as a novice, having studied at the abbey in Metten. As a monk he had the name Em-

Rev. Emmeran Bliemel, O.S.B.

meran. He would become Saint Vincent's most melancholy connection with a decisive event in world history, the American Civil War. Had that war ended differently, the Mason-Dixon Line would now be an international border.

As a priest Bliemel served in parishes in western Pennsylvania before being sent to Covington, Kentucky. In 1860 he went to serve the German parish of the Assumption in Nashville, Tennessee. A photograph of Bliemel shows him in a clerical suit, his hair unruly and his face boyish, and recollections handed down describe him as a quiet man. He had shown gifts in mathematics and logic, as well as an ability to master English. When in April, 1861, the South opened fire on the American military at Fort Sumter, South Carolina, civil war ensued. Bliemel joined the Tenth Tennessee Infantry as a chaplain. In August, 1864, while hearing the confession of a wounded colonel during the battle of Jonesboro, Georgia, Bliemel was killed by cannon fire. He was the only Catholic chaplain to lose his life in that war.

Archabbot Boniface Krug, O.S.B.

BONIFACE KRUG

Among the students at Saint Vincent when Pius IX issued *Inter ceteras* was the young monk, Boniface Krug.[32] Born in 1838 near Fulda, Germany, Herman Krug came to America as a boy with his parents; they settled in Baltimore, where they met Boniface Wimmer. In 1849 Krug came to Saint Vincent for school; in 1851 he entered the novitiate of the monastery, receiving the name Boniface. Ten years later he was ordained priest by the bishop of Pittsburgh, and Krug celebrated his first Mass in Baltimore.

Upon his return to Saint Vincent, Krug served as director (today called president) of the College. In 1862, Wimmer sent Krug to teach at Assumption College, in Sandwich, Ontario. Wimmer sought to avoid having Krug and other talented monks drafted into the Union army. The United Sates government, not surprisingly, regarded Krug as a draft-dodger, and he was legally unable to return to Pennsylvania. Since Krug was a monk in solemn vows, bound under canon law to his monastery, a solution acceptable to at least canon, if not civil, law was in order. Wimmer approved of Krug leaving Canada for Italy, there to transfer his vows to the monastery of Monte Cassino, which Saint Benedict had established and where he had been buried. Krug had a gift for languages, mastering English, German, Italian, and Latin, and he soon became a fixture at Monte Cassino, serving as guest master for foreign visitors.

In 1869 Krug as guest master showed Benedictine hospitality to a small group of Americans from New England. Henry Wadsworth Longfellow was sixty-two and America's most famous poet. He had taught modern languages, first at his alma mater, Bowdoin, then at Harvard; his classical education gave him the intellectual skills to compose epics in hexameter using American themes, such as *Evangeline* (1849) and *The Song of Hiawatha* (1858). His shorter poems, such as "The Village Blacksmith" (1841) and "Paul Revere's Ride" (1863), were required to be memorized and recited by American school children into the 1970s. His carol, "I heard the bells on Christmas Day," inspired by the American Civil War, is still sung. In 1867 he had published his translation into English of Dante's *Divina Commedia*, and Longfellow decided to visit once again his beloved Italy. A man of means and leisure, he took his family with him, part of their tour bringing them to Monte Cassino.

In 1875 Longfellow published in *The Atlantic Monthly* a poem about Monte Cassino, and in it he refers obliquely to Boniface Krug.[33] Longfellow recalls the day in March six years before, when a wood fire in the chapter room took the chill off their meandering conversation. Longfellow and Krug sat and discussed Saint Benedict and monastic history, as well as the criticisms of monastic life made by Giovanni Boccaccio, who in the fourteenth century spoke for all those across the ages who see monks as men running away from life in order to be lazy under the pretense of prayer. "Upon such themes as these," Longfellow writes in his poem, "with one young friar/I sat conversing late into the night."[34] Poetic license permits calling a monk a friar; it rhymes with "fire." Historical imagination conjures with two American accents, one with echoes of ancestral East Anglia, the other with perhaps a trace of native German; two men thirty-one years apart in age but brought together by a shared love for Christian culture and that sublime medieval invention, the fireplace.

Longfellow's sister, Anna Longfellow Pierce, kept a diary of the trip. She describes their ascent by donkey to the abbey, and she notes the courtesy of two monks. "One of the brothers," she writes, "a very charming and handsome American from Pennsylvania and another older Italian…with shrugging shoulders and folded hands, sat by to talk with us while we ate."[35] Presumably the monk from Pennsylvania was Boniface Krug. She also records her brother studying the monastery's prized manuscript of Dante, and a recently published copy of it being presented to him by the abbot.

Longfellow and his family mounted their donkeys and went down from the mountain monastery, thence by steam locomotive to Naples. Krug returned to his duties as guest master, but not forever. In 1874 the abbot made him prior of the abbey, and in 1888 the Benedictines of the abbey of Cesena elected Krug their abbot. Seven years later, the abbots of the Cassinese Congregation of Benedictine monks elected Krug their abbot president, and in 1897 the monks of Monte Cassino chose Krug to be their new archabbot, being numbered the 296th successor to Saint Benedict. Among Krug's achievements as archabbot was the not inconsiderable one of replacing chamber pots with flush toilets.

For all his success as a churchman, Krug's years in Italy did not erase his memories of America. In 1908, a year before his death, he returned to visit Saint Vincent. Krug was remembered as having "a gentle and kindly disposition" and being "a pleasing singer, an accomplished musician."[36] Perhaps these gifts of kindness and harmony help explain his ability to earn the respect of a variety of people, from Catholic abbots, not least being the hard to please Boniface Wimmer, to Protestants such as the Longfellows.

REGIS CANEVIN

Down the hill from the growing complex at Saint Vincent was a cluster of buildings forming the village of Beatty. It had a post office, later transferred to nearby Latrobe as the latter grew into a small borough and Beatty remained a dusty crossroads settlement. Both Beatty and Latrobe were home to several Presbyterian families of Scots and northern Irish descent, and also in Beatty were a few families of Catholic Irish. Among these families were the Canevins.[37] In 1839, Thomas Canevin and his wife, Roseanna Larkin Canevin, had come to the United States from Ireland, Castle Dawson in County Derry, to be precise. They had first settled in Ohio, but in 1852 they moved to Pittsburgh. By the next year they had left Pittsburgh for Beatty, where they were tenant farmers on land owned by the Sisters of Mercy, operators of a girls boarding school, Saint Xavier's Academy.

On this rented farm in 1853, John Francis Regis Canevin was born the eighth child of Thomas and Roseanna Canevin. He grew up in Beatty, and as a boy he saw the emergence of the monastery and schools next to the old parish of Saint Vincent. From the village in the valley of the Loyalhanna, a monastery on a hill could not be hid. In 1872 Regis Canevin began attending Saint Vincent College, and in 1876 he entered the Seminary. In 1879 he was ordained to the priesthood for the Diocese of Pittsburgh.

Tall, lean, and dignified, Canevin was also a modest and reticent man. Once, when invited to give the commencement address at his alma mater, he wrote to a friend, "Just think of *me* appearing before the venerable faculty and learned students of St. Vincent's."[38] From boyhood, the example around him had been one of steady, substantial work. His parents had their hands full with a farm and a family, and the Sisters of Mercy at Saint Xavier's were kept busy running their school. Moreover, the Benedictine monks at Saint Vincent were working to build a monastery, as well as a college and a seminary. While the lay brothers farmed and constructed sturdy brick buildings, the priests taught and served in parishes. It is not too much to see these exemplars impressing themselves upon the mind of the young Canevin. His adult life was marked by fatherly sacrifice, priestly ministry, and relentless construction.

As bishop of Pittsburgh he was noted for his building projects. In 1903, when Canevin became co-adjutor bishop of Pittsburgh, all of western Pennsylvania had a quarter of a million Catholics; by 1921, when he retired, the city of Pittsburgh alone had that number of Catholics.[39] To serve these people, many of them new to America and striving like Sysiphus to keep body and soul together, Canevin built 134 new churches and schools, and he added five new hospitals to the existing three. He also built the De Paul Institute, a school for poor children who were deaf, blind, or impaired of speech. In the midst of the grueling pace Canevin set for planning, fund-raising, and prayer, "he never cared to be exploited as a personality."[40] One can see why such a quiet man would notice the plight of the members of his flock who were like the man Jesus healed in the Decapolis (Mark 7:31-37).

Canevin's crowning glory as a builder remains Saint Paul's Cathedral, completed in 1906. In 1855, the original Saint Paul's of Pittsburgh, a Gothic structure on Grant's Hill, had burnt to the ground; its successor was also in the Gothic style. In 1901, after much deliberation, the Irish-born Bishop Richard Phelan sold it to Protestant philanthropist Henry Clay Frick. Phelan's plan was to use the money from Frick for a new cathedral, to be built in more expansive proportions in a more spacious part of the steel city.

Bishop J.F. Regis Canevin

Two years later, Canevin, as Phelan's co-adjutor bishop, laid the cornerstone of the new cathedral, in the city's Oakland neighborhood, at the corner of Fifth Avenue and Craig Street. It is thus not far from the University of Pittsburgh, with its lawns and trees. This new church rose quickly, a striking example of neo-Gothic architecture in the French style. Its exterior is of Indiana limestone, its interior of stone and wood. The high altar is carved from Carrara marble, and oaken pews and wainscoting soften what could be a stark but lofty chamber. Stained glass windows depict saints and biblical scenes while admitting sunlight through rich blues, reds, and greens. Not only did this choice of architectural styles connect the new cathedral with its predecessors, it kept continuity with centuries of Catholic culture.[41]

The new cathedral was consecrated in October, 1906. Participating in its consecration were eight prelates, including Bishop Leo Haid, Vicar Apostolic of North Carolina and abbot of the Benedictine abbey in Belmont, North Carolina. Haid, four years Canevin's senior, was also a native of the neighborhood around Latrobe. In 1872, after his priestly ordination, he served as a professor and chaplain at Saint Vincent College, where Canevin was a student. Although the idea for a new cathedral had begun with Bishop Phelan, his deteriorating health made necessary in 1903 a co-adjutor bishop; in 1904 illness took Phelan from this life. Thus, Saint Paul's Cathedral is Canevin's monument, "and the bronze tablet that was unveiled at his funeral [in 1927], after the medieval manner shows the Bishop with the cathedral in his arms."[42]

In October, 1920, the Seminary invited Canevin to address "a short allocution to the Seminarians."[43] Canevin was always welcome at Saint Vincent, not only because he was a distinguished alumnus, but also because in 1914 he had declared the Seminary the official school of theology for the Diocese of Pittsburgh. In the words of the *St. Vincent College Journal,* Canevin spoke "from the fountain of long experience in dealing with young Levites from the seminary."[44] He encouraged the seminarians to "strive to be an *Alter Christus,*" in order to become "the light of the world and the salt of the earth."[45] He exhorted them to self-denial, after the example of the saints, reminding them that they should have "this singleness of purpose, the glorification of God and the salvation of souls."[46] Denial of self and holiness of life for the sake of God were not original ideas with Canevin, and he underscored his source. "The authority of the seminary," he said, "is the authority of the Church, and the authority of the Church is that of God."[47]

The students knew their bishop to practice what he preached. In 1921, Canevin was in his late sixties and exhausted. He resigned as bishop and retired to serve as a chaplain in a convent. Upon his resignation, the College journal editorialized on his dedication to the Church. "During the sixteen years of his episcopacy," the editorial noted, Canevin "had literally spent himself, worn himself out in the interests of the souls committed to his jurisdiction."[48] His "unstinting forgetfulness of self," as well as his "boundless but quiet enthusiasm"[49] had made their mark upon the students at Saint Vincent.

SETTING THE PACE

The early alumni of the Seminary served the Church in America and Europe, in parishes, in monasteries, and on the field of battle. They took part in the great events of the day, whether civil war or building cathedrals. With each decade, Saint Vincent Seminary would continue to produce parish priests—some unsung, others becoming bishops—as well as monks ordained to the priesthood. These priests, whether religious or diocesan, turned their talents and their vocations to a variety of services to the Church and the world. There emerged historians and musicians, labor priests and scholars of Scripture. What concerned the people of God also concerned priests from Saint Vincent.

All the while, Boniface Wimmer was at the center of major events as well. From Saint Vincent he sent priests and brothers to the Mid-west, and both before and after the American Civil War, into the South, by 1887 founding six abbeys. In 1888 in Rome there began Collegio di Sant' Anselmo, the international school for Benedictines; its planning had been among the last of Wimmer's acts. At the time of his death he had approved ventures in Ecuador and New Hampshire. The papal bull *Inter ceteras* of 1855 formed his abbeys into the American Cassinese Congregation of the Order of Saint Benedict. Wimmer was the Congregation's first abbot president, and in that role he was in 1869 summoned by the pope to Rome.

2

FAITH AND REASON

On a drizzly December morning in 1869, more than seven hundred prelates of the Roman Catholic Church processed down the *Scala Regia* into the nave of Saint Peter's Basilica in Rome.[50] Leading the procession, as protocol demanded, was an abbot, Boniface Wimmer; at the end of the majestic train was the papal *sedia gestatoria* bearing aloft Pope Pius IX. It was a day of splendor, full of color and song. Swiss Guards in polished helmets and blue and orange uniforms first designed, some say, by Michelangelo himself, snapped to attention with their halberds. In the midst of the chanting of the ninth-century hymn, *Veni Creator Spiritus,* mitred prelates from Wimmer to the pope shone chryselephantine in vestments of white and gold, befitting the occasion. The first ecumenical council of the Vatican had begun.

Debate was difficult, given the poor acoustics of the hall.[51] While this feature of architecture frustrated some participants, it did not deter them. To an Anglican journalist used to observing the British Parliament, an ecumenical council was an impressive idea. "The

EMINENTISSIMI ET REVERENDISSIMI DOMINI
S. E. R. CARDINALES
REVERENDISSIMI DOMINI
PATRIARCHÆ PRIMATES ARCHIEPISCOPI EPISCOPI

ABBATES NULLIUS DICECESIS
SUPREMI ORDINUM REGULARIUM MODERATORES
QUI CONCILIO ŒCUMENICO VATICANO INTERFUERUNT

Photo Album Title Page of Vatican I Participants

Council, with its 900 members collected from every country in the world," wrote Walter Bagehot in *The Economist*, "is the oldest and widest representative body in the history of mankind."[52] In those days before a League of Nations or United Nations, Bagehot saw a secular, political dimension to a council of the Church. "[T]he Council is even now the only body," he said, "which claims or attempts to carry out the representation of the whole human race, without distinction of country, language, allegiance, or colour."[53] He expanded his point, describing the Council as "the parliament of the universal Church," composed of prelates convened "to represent with considerable accuracy almost all the forms of thought still considered orthodox by faithful believers."[54]

Bagehot was an admirer of the writings of John Henry Newman, although he was baffled by Newman's spiritual growth from Anglicanism to Catholicism. Both Bagehot and Newman were of a mind with an Irishman of the eighteenth century, Edmund Burke, who saw wisdom in slow, organic change over time; an ecumenical council, with its deliberative nature, seemed to be a means to such an end. Even people casually aware of the news of the day saw that a council discussing what was held orthodox by "faithful believers" could not be sectarian.

To his credit, Pope Pius IX followed the example of the Council of Trent and invited Protestants to the Vatican Council. Charles Hodge, a Philadelphian who taught Calvinist theology at Princeton, replied. Writing in behalf of his denomination in America, Hodge sent regrets, explaining courteously why Presbyterians, at least, could not accept the papal invitation. After citing disagreements over such tenets as tradition and apostolic succession, Hodge expressed a desire to live in charity with all. "We regard as Christian brethren," Hodge wrote, "all who worship, love, and obey him [Christ] as their God and Saviour."[55] At the Council a bishop who put in a good word for Protestants was heckled by his brother bishops. So, Catholic dialogue with the separated brethren awaited another day.

DOGMATIC CONSTITUTIONS

The First Vatican Council produced two notable documents, both dogmatic constitutions: *Dei Filius* ("The Son of God"), and *Pastor Aeternus* ("The Eternal Shepherd"). *Dei Filius* reminds the Church of timeless truths about divine revelation, especially in Scripture, as well as the relation between faith and reason. *Pastor Aeternus* defines the belief that the bishop of Rome, when speaking on faith or morals *ex cathedra,* from the chair of Saint Peter, that is, with apostolic authority, speaks infallibly. As dogmatic constitutions of the faith, both conciliar documents are essential for the life and growth of the Church.

Boniface Wimmer stood foursquare behind the Council defining the concept of papal infallibility on faith and morals; he called that definition "necessary" for priests to defend and protect dogma against rationalists.[56] Although Protestants, Orthodox, and dissenting Catholics have from 1870 to the present balked at the dogmatic constitution *Pastor Aeternus,* their qualms will not detain us. Pertinent to the history of the Seminary is *Dei Filius* and its teaching on faith and reason. From it grow the standards for seminary education established by the Third Plenary Council of Baltimore, at which Wimmer also played a part. Before looking at the Council of Baltimore, we do well to look at *Dei Filius.*

Wimmer and the other Fathers of Vatican I were concerned with two errors facing the Church. One was an exclusive faith in human reason, the other a blinkered focus on faith alone. "Even

though faith is above reason," *Dei Filius* explains, "there can never be any real disagreement between faith and reason, since it is the same God who reveals the mysteries and infuses faith, and who has endowed the human mind with the light of reason."[57] Furthermore, faith and reason "mutually support each other," and so the Church can promote "the development of human arts and studies."[58] Thus, the Council saw faith and reason going hand in hand, since either one by itself would wander off in an

Archabbot Boniface Wimmer, O.S.B., at Vatican I

48

eccentric orbit.

In the nineteenth century, the Church faced more than speculative misuses of faith and reason. She faced a custom-tailored version of Augustinianism and a tidy set of theorems based upon excavated skeletons. The Church sought a way to steer between the extremes of the Calvinism of Charles Hodge on the one hand, and the extrapolations of Darwinian theory by T. H. Huxley, on the other. While these systems of belief were at first part of Protestant culture, they had a tendency to travel, entering the air breathed also by Jews and Catholics. Priests in America especially would meet with both sets of beliefs, whether belief in science or in faith alone, and they would need not only their own wits about them, but also those of an angelic doctor. The interpretation of Vatican I by one of its Fathers influenced American seminary education, and so to that interpretation we now turn.

INTERPRETING THE COUNCIL

From the statements in *Dei Filius* on faith and reason grew other church documents. An elderly cardinal at the Council, Vincenzo Gioacchino Pecci, in 1878 became Pope Leo XIII, and much of his pontificate went to teaching the Church and the world what the Council meant. In 1879, Leo XIII issued an encyclical letter, *Aeterni Patris,* and in it he answered the question some raised about how to find a reliable guide along the path formed by faith and reason. Leo XIII reminded the Church of Saint Thomas Aquinas and his use of reason to shine light on

Pope Leo XIII

faith, while faith gave reason grounds on which to shine.

The bishops of the United States had met twice in plenary councils to discuss concerns facing the Church in the young republic. These councils had been in 1852 and 1866, convened in Baltimore, the country's primatial see. In 1884 the bishops met in a third plenary council in Baltimore. Present were seven abbots, including Boniface Wimmer. In the course of its four weeks, the Third Plenary Council of Baltimore produced the now famous Baltimore Catechism, and the Council also set a goal of each Catholic parish having its own school. This concern for the religious instruction of the faithful extended also to higher education. The Council set standards for seminary education, and these standards influenced the curriculum at Saint Vincent.

The Council decreed that all major seminaries require the same courses.[59] All seminarians were to have three years of philosophy and four of theology before being ordained to the priesthood. Philosophy included logic, metaphysics, and ethics, as well as the principles of natural law. Theology included moral and dogmatic theology, biblical exegesis, Church history, canon law, liturgy, and homiletics. Exegesis was to use the text of the Vulgate sanctioned by the Council of Trent, and liturgy was to have Gregorian chant. Binding all these studies was to be the Scholastic approach of Thomas Aquinas. To support these decrees, the Acts of the Third Plenary Council cited both *Dei Filius* and *Aeterni Patris.*

From the Council in Baltimore, Wimmer returned to Saint Vincent and set about putting its directives into action. Fourteen years earlier, in April, 1870, the General Assembly of Pennsylvania had incorporated the Seminary, giving it the right in civil law to grant degrees. Bishops and religious superiors, mostly all abbots, who sought a seminary for their men saw in the Saint Vincent of the 1880s and 1890s not only a school recognized by the secular authorities, but also one committed to the authority of Rome. Wimmer set a course for the orthodox way, using the curriculum he helped to shape at Baltimore. A distinguished alumnus from this period was a native of New York, George Mundelein. Years later, when archbishop of Chicago, he spoke to a group of German-Americans, a group he was proud to claim as his own. "If there is one characteristic that stands out in the German people," he told them, "it is their faculty for organization."[60] Mundelein knew this trait from his own family, and from his days at the Saint Vincent of Boniface Wimmer.

END OF AN ERA

In December, 1887, Boniface Wimmer died. He had overseen and nurtured his dream of a Benedictine monastery in America for forty-one often tempestuous years. It is a tribute to Wimmer that his monastery outlived him and flourished. Catholic scholars writing the history of the Church in the United States tend to overlook the role of missionaries from Benedictine monasteries, and so they miss the contribution of Wimmer.[61] By any objective standard, Wimmer, founder of his Order in America, stands alongside the Franciscan, Jesuit, and Redemptorist missionaries who went before him.

Wimmer was inspired by the English Benedictines of the eighth century, intrepid men of prayer who took the Gospel to the pagan woods of Germany. Wimmer kept in mind the commission of Jesus to "Go and teach all nations," and it worried him that Benedictines in Germany, Austria, and Switzerland were so deeply committed to their monastic vow of stability as to become fossilized.[62] It was with this concern uppermost in his mind that to the first Swiss abbot in America, Martin Marty, Wimmer wrote with frustration. Wimmer was surprised the Swiss monks did not "set out with bag and baggage and return" to "a cozy, comfortable life" back home, "just like many of your fellow countrymen who never left the valley where they were born."[63] Although the Swiss monks seemed at first content to live a monastic observance that to Wimmer seemed reclusive, Marty became a bishop in the Dakota territory, where he made a name as a missionary.

Still, it must be said that unlike most historians writing about the Church in America, monks writing about the missions in America can easily put Wimmer and Martin Marty center stage. In defense of those monastic historians, one must note that they tend to write histories of their own monasteries, nearly all deriving from the German Wimmer or the Swiss Marty, and founders loom large.

Perhaps some balance comes from considering that for all his great works for the Church, Wimmer could not have foreseen two events that may have caused him to adapt his plans. In 1893, the American historian Frederick Jackson Turner observed that in the United States, the frontier, what he called "the meeting point between savagery and civilization,"[64] was closed. Once uncharted territory was now settled, and one could not draw a line marking new lands for pioneering. With the dissolving of a sense of frontier soon came a maturing of the Catholic Church in America. In 1908, Pope Pius X determined that the United States was no longer mission territory, and thus canon law governing such missionary lands no longer applied.[65] "Wimmer understood," writes one scholar, "that the Benedictine Order had been successful over the centuries because of its ability to adapt to what it found in every culture."[66] Wimmer had the audacity of an entrepreneur and the grit of a frontiersman. It is unclear how he would have adapted to a land that resembled less the unwashed Germany evangelized by Saint Boniface of Devon than it did the baptized Germany cultivated by the Holy Roman Empire begun by Charlemagne.

HENRY GANSS

Since the days of the Jewish priesthood and the sacrifices of the Temple in Jerusalem, music has been essential to the worship of the God of Abraham. Saint Vincent produced a composer of music for the Church, and to him we now turn. Born in 1855, Henry Ganss grew up in Lancaster, Pennsylvania, his parents having come from Hesse Darmstadt, in Germany.[67] He was thus three years older than Theodore Roosevelt, Columba Marmion, and Katharine Drexel. At the age of thirteen, Ganss's parents sent him to the preparatory school at Saint Vincent. He then entered Saint Vincent College, and from there he entered the Seminary, studying for the Diocese of Harrisburg. In 1876, Ganss received from the College a doctorate in music. In 1878 at the abbey church of Saint Vincent he was ordained priest for the Diocese of Harrisburg.

From 1890 to 1910, Ganss served as pastor of Saint Patrick's Church in Carlisle, Pennsylvania. There he ministered to the Indians of the Carlisle Indian Industrial School, most of the Indians, including the athlete Jim Thorpe, being Catholic. In this work Ganss sought the help of Mother Katharine Drexel, who gave funds towards the building of a new church in 1892. She also built a school beside the church for her Sisters of the Blessed Sacrament to teach the Indians. While engaged in this ministry and that of his parish, Ganss found time to write essays and music. Ganss's literary and musical works helped earn him entries in *The Dictionary of American Biography* and *The New Catholic Encyclopedia,* rare posthumous honors for a parish priest, however hard-working.

By his musical and literary work, Ganss thus proved true a comment by a priest writing in 1890 about the need for more intellectual training in Catholic seminaries. "A Catholic theologian," the priest wrote, "can now hope to gain a hearing and a name in learned circles…in some amateur capacity," not as a theologian, but like "an amateur archaeologist who has had the luck to identify a mummy."[68] Ganss is remembered not so much as a priest as he is for his music and his writing.

Around 1910, while convalescing from the chronic illness that would take his life two tears later, he wrote memoirs of his time at Saint Vincent. Although much of the memoir recalls Ganss's days in the College, one scene from his time in Seminary bears repeating. After Ganss's ordination Mass, with the "holy unction of my ordination still on my hands," Ganss met Boniface Wimmer "in the monastery corridor."[69] Wimmer hurried towards Ganss and addressed him "affectionately by my Christian name;" he wished the new priest "the fullest measure of God's grace in the holy priesthood" and then knelt and asked for Ganss's blessing. Ganss recalled, "I felt the way poor St. Peter felt at the feetwashing on Holy Thursday."

As a composer, Ganss wrote waltzes, a march, and Masses, and in 1900 he published a requiem Mass for Wimmer. It was still the era of orchestral Masses, something Wimmer himself enjoyed, especially when resonant with flutes, horns, and drums. "And when saints like he [sic]," Ganss asked, "came to such conclusions, what could be expected from the rank and file?"[70] One recalls that it was the era of the young Gustav Mahler, who wove into his thunderously elaborate symphonies not only the folk melodies of the southern Germans, but also marches and, on one occasion, the *Veni Creator Spiritus.* Ganss was fond of what was then modern music, works such as those of Richard Wagner and Franz Liszt. For *The Catholic Encyclopedia* of 1910 Ganss wrote the entry on Liszt.

Ganss also wrote the encyclopedia's entry on Martin Luther, about whom he had written six historical articles. Ganss considered Luther a central figure in modern history, and of the more than 5,000 volumes in Ganss's private library, 800 were on Luther. Ganss's fascination with his subject derived from a concern that Luther was rarely treated scientifically. Protestants seemed to compose hagiographies of Luther, while Catholics tended simply to vilify him. Ganss drew upon his historical training and his knowledge of German to write on Luther using texts such as Luther's *Table Talk* in the original.

Felix Fellner

German was the conversational language of Saint Vincent until after the First World War. Even after the death of Wimmer, natives of Germany still came to Saint Vincent to enter monastic life. One of these men was Joseph Fellner, born in Landshut, Bavaria, in 1874,[71] where his father was the chief of police. Joseph had come to the United States in 1893, and in 1894 he enrolled in Saint Vincent College. In 1895 he entered the novitiate at Saint Vincent, where he received the name Felix. He had attended *Gymnasium* in Landshut, receiving a classical education, and he studied theology at Saint Vincent. Ordained priest in 1901, he served at a parish before teaching in the Seminary. That career began in 1909 and continued until his retirement in 1954. He died in 1963 in the monastery infirmary.

In the Seminary, Fellner taught Church history; in the College, modern history. He is remembered for lecturing in English with a heavy German accent and noticeable German syntax. He was also noted for his dry wit, such as when lecturing on

Newly-ordained Rev. Felix Fellner, O.S.B.

the Protestant Reformation in England. "She was called the Virgin Queen," he said of Elizabeth I, "und as a queen she was successful."

While he is remembered mainly as an interesting professor of Church history, Fellner also wrote history, although no major work attaches to his name. In 1905, to mark the dedication of the new archabbey church (now known as the basilica), Fellner published *St. Vincenz Gemeinde und Erzabtei,* a work showing the market at the time for historical books in German. Near the end of his career, in 1956, he compiled *Abbot Boniface and his Monks,* a typescript printed by the Archabbey Press, bound in five volumes, and distributed privately. He once asked a colleague on the English faculty of the College to proofread an article he planned to submit to a journal. When the heavily re-written draft returned, Fellner sighed and said, "It is no longer history!"

Of Fellner's handful of articles in scholarly journals and entries in *The Dictionary of American Biography,* some deal with Wimmer or topics of local history in western Pennsylvania. Worth noting is a study of the twelfth-century Cistercian, Otto of Freising. Otto was bishop of Freising, Bavaria, and he wrote a history, *Historia de duabus Civitatibus,* often called the *Chronicon.* In Fellner's article we see a confluence of Fellner's interests in Church history and in local history, in this case local to his early years in Bavaria. While assessing the philosophy of history found in Otto's work, and noting Otto's differences from Saint Augustine's *De Civitate Dei,* Fellner gives his own view of history, or rather the writing of history.

Fellner contrasts the scientific historian of his day, who proceeds "almost like a doctor who performs an autopsy," with the medieval historian, who had foremost in his mind "the whole living organism of a body politic or ecclesiastic, as directed by an all-ruling Providence."[72] Fellner saw the virtue in balance between the two methods. "Christian ethics and the canons of true science," he said, "demand a proportionate share as the subject itself dictates."[73] Fellner praises Otto's work for having "the first quality which every historical treatise should possess," namely, "the earnest aim of the writer to be truthful."[74] Here we see Felix Fellner, monk and historian, balancing science and faith, always striving for truth.

TURNING THE CENTURY

As the nineteenth century waned, the population of Catholics in the United States grew. Wimmer's original vision of ministering to German Catholic immigrants had already given way to the reality of ministering also to the large number of Irish Catholics in America. Broadly speaking, from the days of Leo XIII until at least those of Pius XII, the story of Saint Vincent Seminary can be seen as one of parallel lives, German monks studying for the priesthood alongside Irish diocesan candidates.

Among the latter were several who became bishops, such as Hugh C. Boyle, sixth bishop of Pittsburgh. A native of Johnstown, Pennsylvania, he was a student at the Seminary in the late 1880s.[75] At the end of May, 1889, a heavy summer rain storm weakened the earthen dam at the South Fork Fishing and Hunting Club, and the dam burst, causing the tragedy known as the Johnstown Flood. "At Latrobe, at

Bishop Boyle (left) and Rev. Felix Fellner, O.S.B.

Bishops Boyle and Canevin

the foot of Chestnut Ridge," writes David McCullough, "the Loyalhanna was twice its normal size and well over its banks."[76] When
news of the devastation of Johnstown reached Saint Vincent, Boyle
walked home, a distance of thirty-five miles. When he arrived at the
ruined city, he learned that his father, four brothers, and his three
sisters were among the dead. Only his mother and a baby brother
survived.

After the flood, however, the city of Johnstown was rebuilt, and
families picked up the pieces of their broken lives. For Catholics,
it was an experience like that of Noah. Not only had Catholics in
America crossed the waters of the Atlantic, they had passed through
the waters of a flood that was both historic and symbolic. Catholics
in western Pennsylvania emerged from the flood having preserved
the rich variety of life from the old world, not least being the wisdom

of Thomas Aquinas, and they came into the sunshine of a new day, and a new century, to build new altars and make present again the sacrifice of Calvary.

Diocesan Seminarians ca. 1907

3

ARCHITECTURE AND SCHOLASTICISM

By 1900, the United States was emerging as a formidable player upon the world stage. National leadership remained within the clubby circles of old families along the eastern seaboard. President William McKinley, wily yet avuncular, was re-elected in 1900, his running-mate being Theodore Roosevelt, a brash young member of a family long part of the New York described in the novels of Edith Wharton. McKinley had served as an officer in the Union army during the American Civil War, and as president he had prosecuted America's war with Spain, a conflict seen by some as symbolic of the struggle between Protestantism and Catholicism. As a result of that war, America gained control over Catholic islands such as Cuba and the Philippines.

In 1901, while greeting people in Buffalo, New York, William McKinley was assassinated by an anarchist from Poland, Leon Czolgosz. For Protestants in America, most living in the small towns that had helped elect McKinley, this murder confirmed fears of foreigners, especially foreigners from Catholic countries. It was a period of vast Catholic immigration from Europe. Between 1870 and 1920, the number of Catholics in America rose from seven million to twenty million, and the number of Catholic priests from seven thousand to twenty thousand.[77] As the Catholic population of the country grew, as the number of men responding to priestly vocations increased, seminaries expanded as well.

During this period of growth, the Church faced a challenge from within. Catholic scholars, many of them priests, were applying the intellectual approach of the eighteenth century to Sacred Scripture and Church history. All puzzles of the past, all mysteries of faith, seemed soluble by the cold light of human reason. New insights about language, new discoveries of archaeology, new theories of human development, all were brought to bear on religion, especially Christianity.

In the first decades of the twentieth century, the name foremost on the list of such scholars was a French priest, Alfred Loisy. In 1902 he had published *L'Évangile et l'Église,* a study of the relation between the Gospel and the Church. Loisy concluded that Jesus had expected an imminent coming of the Kingdom of God, but when it seemed not to be forthcoming, Jesus decided to set up a church. This provisional and improvised nature of the Church ran counter to her self-understanding. Loisy, as a priest, continued to write and challenge centuries of Church teaching; when the Pontifical Biblical Commission studied his works and asked him to revise them, he refused. In 1908 he was declared excommunicate.

At Saint Vincent, progress seemed safest along a path clearly marked. The guidance given by Leo XIII in *Aeterni Patris* held sway; until the late 1960s, the alpine clarity of Thomas Aquinas formed the core of the curriculum. As he had centuries before, Aquinas provided nineteenth- and twentieth-century seekers after truth with hope. "To a generation beset by uncertainty and surrounded by incalculable dangers," wrote Sir Richard Southern, "he offered safety and certainty."[78] Aquinas did so by demonstrating "to men struggling with confusion" that there was "the possibility of systematic and clear-cut theological statements."[79] Catholics in America in those days, feeling encircled by poverty and persecution, identified with the insecurities their ancestors had faced. Aquinas lucidly showed that faith was not a relic of "dark ages," but rather a perennial appeal to man's intellect, will, and memory.

Moreover, Aquinas and his school of thought mirrored the position of American Catholics, especially seminarians. Anton Pegis has referred to the ambivalence of Scholastic thought. By that phrase he reminds us that "medieval philosophy was both a Christian philosophy and an instrument of Christian theology."[80] As the Catholic seminarian of the early twentieth century struggled with being a loyal American and being a faithful Catholic, he also grappled with intellectual tools that worked both with faith and with reason.

Students at Saint Vincent Seminary responded to the Thomistic curriculum with enthusiasm, forming the Saint Thomas Literary

 and Homiletic Society. It enjoyed sufficient membership, competing with other clubs, including one focusing on William Shakespeare, that it had three subsets, or "divisions," determined by the language groups of the seminarians, English, German, or Slovak. From 1918 to 1931 members of the Society edited a yearbook, *The Seminarists' Symposium*. They chose as its motto a line often attributed to Saint Augustine: *In Necessariis Unitas, In Dubiis Libertas, In Omnibus Caritas,* "In essential matters, unity; in debatable matters, freedom; in all things, charity."

PONTIFICAL STATUS

Archabbot Leander Schnerr, O.S.B.

Jerome Oetgen has observed that for many bishops and abbots in the United States, this atmosphere of Thomism made Saint Vincent a safe and orthodox seminary.[81] As the reputation of the Seminary grew, Archabbot Leander Schnerr, second successor to Wimmer, mulled over an idea.[82] In November, 1911, he wrote to one of his priests, Ambrose Kohlbeck, a native of Bohemia who since 1907 had been teaching dogmatic theology at Sant' Anselmo, the Benedictine college in Rome. Schnerr asked Kohlbeck to make inquiries in Rome about the viability of the Seminary granting ecclesiastical degrees in philosophy and theology. Hitherto, degrees were seen as unnecessary, a man's ordination to priesthood being the culmination of his years in seminary.

In January, 1912, Schnerr had a reply from Kohlbeck. The right people at the Vatican liked the idea. Kohlbeck included suggestions he had been given by a cardinal for a petition for the right to confer degrees. Schnerr consulted with Bishop Canevin, who agreed to support Schnerr's petition to Rome. Schnerr then wrote to Abbot Leo Haid and Joseph Schrembs, an alumnus of the Seminary and bishop of Toledo, Ohio. These prelates concurred with Canevin, and Schnerr was confident their backing would improve the chances of his petition being considered.

Two years later, in March, 1914, Pope Pius X issued a brief granting Schnerr's request. For the next seven years, Saint Vincent Seminary had the authority to grant ecclesiastical degrees. Seminarians could thus apply for three degrees in sacred theology, the bachelor's, the license, or the doctorate. Each degree required studies in Thomistic philosophy and examinations written in Latin. The doctorate also required oral examinations in Latin.

The new status had an immediate result; in 1914, Bishop Canevin declared Saint Vincent to be the official seminary of the Diocese of Pittsburgh. In 1921, Pope Benedict XV agreed to renew the pontifical status of the Seminary. This renewal would expire in ten years. While this status gave the Seminary distinction, bishops began to doubt its practicality. They needed pastors in parishes, not scholars of philosophy. If a man showed great intellectual promise, like the young Fulton J. Sheen in Peoria, already making a name for himself, he could be sent to the Catholic Universities in Louvain, Rome, or Washington.

By 1930 the world was sharply altered from ten years before; Bishop Canevin and Archabbot Leander were both gone. Moreover, the Great Depression made bishops even more conscious of spending money for education wisely. These concerns over money and scholarly credentials several bishops shared with the new archabbot, Alfred Koch, and Father Ambrose Kohlbeck, the rector. When 1931 and renewal of pontifical status approached, the decision was made with reluctance not to apply for renewal.

Rev. Ambrose Kohlbeck, O.S.B.

RECTORS

Although Demetrius di Marogna had borne the title of rector of the Seminary, after him the Seminary functioned *de facto* as a department of the College. A monk priest teaching in the College was designated to serve also as "director" of the Seminary, an assignment that often changed annually. Catalogues for the College from the latter nineteenth and early twentieth centuries list the Seminary as though it were a faculty of theology. When in 1914 the Seminary received pontifical status, the head of the school became the rector, independent of the College.

Archabbot Leander Schnerr appointed Father Vitus Kratzer, O. S. B., to be the first rector of the pontifical seminary.[83] Kratzer had been born in 1873 in Berg, Bavaria; after studying at the seminary in Eichstätt, in 1891 he came to the United States. Doctors believed a change of climate would improve Kratzer's frail health. Two years later he entered the novitiate at Saint Vincent and followed the usual course to priesthood. In 1899 he was ordained priest, and in 1903 he was sent to Sant' Anselmo. There he studied theology and canon

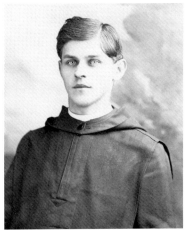

Rev. Vitus Kratzer, O.S.B.

law, receiving a doctorate in the latter. Upon returning to Saint Vincent, he taught canon law and dogmatic theology in the Seminary. Bishop Canevin asked him to serve as a *censor librorum* and member of the diocesan Vigilance Commission against Modernism.

Kratzer was "frank, unpretentious, plain and simple in his manner, outspoken almost to a fault,"[84] fluent in English, German, and Latin. His tenure as rector was brief; after two years his struggle with pernicious anemia forced him to seek treatment, first at a clinic in Chicago, then among the rarefied blue skies of Pueblo, Colorado. Doctors believed the change in climate would restore his failing health. There in November, 1916, he passed away. He was succeeded as rector by Father Ambrose Kohlbeck, who took the helm as the United States drew closer to war.

FIRST WORLD WAR

In June, 1914, the crown prince of the Austro-Hungarian Empire, Archduke Franz Ferdinand, was assassinated in Sarajevo. From that murder uncoiled tensions that led within weeks to what was then called the Great War, now known as the First World War. While the United States remained neutral for the first three years of that war, the war had an effect on seminarians. German submarines made ships on the Atlantic sitting ducks, and the participation of Italy in the war, first on one side, then another, made study in Rome difficult. When in 1915 the Italian government went to war with Austria, the Vatican closed schools such as Sant' Anselmo.

Saint Vincent made the decision to move its seminarians who were in Rome to Fribourg, Switzerland. These seminarians were John Nepomucene Hruza, Francis Mersinger, and Bernardine Pendl.[85] Had they wondered what to expect, a perusal of *The Catholic Encyclopedia* of 1910 would have told them of a fairly young university, founded in 1890. Pope Leo XIII had put the faculty of theology in the care of the Dominicans, and a steady stream of American students had already led to the formation of a society called Columbia. The three students from Saint Vincent obtained pontifical degrees and returned home, all three to teach in the Seminary. When the Great War ended, they found that enrollment at the Seminary continued to be over a hundred, and accommodations for that number were inadequate.

Dedication of Aurelius Hall, June 17, 1923

A New Building

This need and desire to build a new building was part of a wider trend. Catholic dioceses, parishes, and religious houses across America were raising money and breaking ground for new schools, hospitals, and churches. Joel Rippinger has described this so-called "brick and mortar" Catholicism as "the intense effort of the Church…to construct a network of institutions and edifices whose sheer number and size would reflect the solid and permanent presence of Catholics in the United States."[86] Saint Vincent was part of this network, since so many parishes and monasteries derived from it. "Since the late nineteenth century," writes Philip Jenkins, "a number of vigorous and obvious Catholic centers had emerged in Pennsylvania in a belt stretching from St. Marys in Elk County to the great monastery of Latrobe in Westmoreland County."[87] The circle widened beyond Pennsylvania, rippling across such prairie states as Kansas and Minnesota.

From the first days of monastic life at Saint Vincent, accommodations were improvised. The old parish had new life, and new buildings were needed. "Since St. Vincent was just one big family at the start," Anselm Ober reminds us, "there were no separated quarters for various divisions of the community."[88] Until 1877, the Seminary occupied space in college buildings, and seminarians in some years had to fit in wherever there was room. "On account of the overcrowding of the dormitory by reason of the presence of so many students," one collegian recorded in his diary in December, 1867, "and the upper dormitory not yet completed, some beds are placed in the corridor," so that "the Theologians [seminarians] are occupying the beds in the large rooms."[89] The building of 1877, now called Placid Hall, was the first building at Saint Vincent designated for the Seminary, with "study halls…on the second floor and the dormitory on the third."[90] Thirty years later, the construction of what is now known as Alfred Hall again changed the scenery and the situation of

Ordination Class of 1918

Archabbot Aurelius Stehle, O.S.B.

the Seminary, occupying "the second and third floors of this building."[91] Until the 1950s, seminary classes were held in Alfred Hall.

In June, 1921, Archabbot Aurelius Stehle laid the cornerstone of the new seminary building.[92] Before being elected abbot, Stehle had taught Latin and Greek in the Seminary, and in 1915 he published a manual on liturgy, a work still consulted by masters of ceremonies. Stehle's work of reference compiled longstanding customs, and it buttressed Saint Vincent's reputation for rubrical correctness. While a Swiss-American monastery such as Conception Abbey got attention partaking of the heady fare of the liturgical movement, Saint Vincent's offering was as safe and standard as meat and potatoes.

Still, Stehle the author was known mainly to specialists in a limited field. "The most important contribution of Archabbot Aurelius," said Paulinus Selle, "to St. Vincent's external and internal development was the erection of the magnificent dormitory for the seminarians."[93] This building remained the primary home of the Seminary for nearly thirty years. After the Second World War, new quarters for the Seminary allowed this structure of 1923 to be renamed for Archabbot Aurelius.

The new Seminary building was tall and lean, a red brick structure roughly 170 feet by 40 feet, soaring up six stories.[94] Rising as it does on the slope of a hill, it still presents a stately figure. "An inviting appearance is added," Selle remarked, "to the otherwise somewhat blank front of the building by the heavily arched doorway and the front porch."[95] The blankness of this front was also reduced by two niches, one holding a statue of Saint Benedict, the other of Saint Thomas Aquinas, symbolizing the Patristic and Scholastic inheritance of the Seminary. Benedictines also are fond of pointing out that

Aurelius Hall

as a boy Aquinas studied at Monte Cassino.

Inside, the new seminary building offered around 180 rooms for seminarians and six suites for officials. Oak woodwork was lumbered on the monastery's wood lots on Chestnut Ridge; cypress trim came from a mill in Pittsburgh. Each floor had wash rooms, as well as "a sanitary drinking fountain," a bonus deriving from "the accidental finding of a spring when excavation was being made."[96] Rooms were twelve by nine feet, with closet and sink, and flooring was tile or terrazzo, presciently resistant to fire.

A student who knew that building not long after its construction has left his recollections of it. From 1930 to 1934, Charles Owen Rice was a student at the Seminary. A native of Pittsburgh, he had

Msgr. Charles Owen Rice

studied at Duquesne University, and he distinguished himself in his priestly ministry by helping members of labor unions. In 1992, after giving a guest lecture at the Seminary, he wrote some recollections of his days as a seminarian.

Rice recalled a pleasant day in 1932 and a fellow seminarian returning from a walk, an old branch serving as his walking stick. Rice had a pocket knife and offered to cut the rough spots off of the stick. The floors of the seminary's rooms, Rice remembered, were "of a substance that wears like iron and is fireproof."[97] Rice's whittling produced a pile of shavings, and the floor's dust pan and brush were not handy. "What seemed like a sensible idea at the time," Rice recorded, "was a small fire in the middle of the floor." Rice opened the window and set the dried bits of wood ablaze.

Unfortunately for Rice, another seminarian stopped by for a visit. He was not bothered by the fire, but when Rice's door opened, wood smoke escaped into the hallway. The next day Rice was asked to report to the rector, Father Nepomucene Hruza. Up to this point, Rice had not been a problem student. Rice remembered Hruza as "stern of mien and unflappable," and Rice imagined the rector "must have been secretly amused" by the fire.[98] Moreover, Hruza "did not explode" as Rice "respectfully noted that I had not broken any of the rules in our manual."[99] Here the foolishness of youth and the wisdom of age met, neither the worse for wear.

DAILY LIFE

A student in Rice's day followed a tight schedule.[100] Classes met six days a week, with none on Wednesday or Saturday afternoons. A typical weekday began officially at five in the morning, and by 5:20 all were to be assembled for Morning Prayer. Mass followed, then breakfast. Classes began at eight, and the mid-day meal was at 11:10, and until 1:30 students were free for adoration of the Blessed Sacrament and then in recreation. From 1:30 to 2:15 was time for studying, and then classes resumed. There was community recreation at four and lasting half an hour, immediately followed by spiritual reading in the chapel. At quarter to five the books closed, and the seminarians said the Rosary. The evening meal was at five, and afterwards was more time before the Blessed Sacrament and in recreation. At seven began an hour and three quarters of study time, ended with Night Prayer at quarter to nine, with lights out at nine-thirty.

According to Seminary catalogues from the 1920s and 1930s, seminarians from dioceses were required to wear black cassocks and black cinctures. Also required were birettas. When on business in Latrobe, for example, a black suit and black necktie were required; after receiving holy orders, a black suit and a Roman collar, always with an appropriate hat. Recreation took various forms depending upon the weather. In warmer months, some seminarians went to the field north of the cemetery, there to play volleyball or baseball. Since canon law required them to wear cassocks on campus, they did so until reaching the field, where they removed the cassocks and revealed lay clothes underneath. During the colder seasons, recreation was indoors, often taking the form of that medieval diversion, playing cards.

JAMES R. COX

An alumnus who made his mark in the 1920s and 1930s was a member of the Class of 1911, James R. Cox.[101] Cox's activities influenced those of Rice, although the two men took different angles on helping the worker who was being treated like a beast of burden. Cox had worked a series of odd jobs before studying for the priesthood, and he knew the difficulty of making ends meet. During the First World War he served with a hospital unit in France; upon his return, he became a hospital chaplain in Pittsburgh.

James R. Cox as an Army chaplain.

A portly man with rimless spectacles, Cox was described by *Time* magazine as the "plump priest who once led a 'jobless army' to Washington."[102] The reference was to Cox's efforts to help the unemployed people of Pittsburgh. In 1932 Cox left Pittsburgh for Washington, D. C., with forty-five thousand marchers; along the way, which took them through Harrisburg, roughly thirty-thousand straggled back home. Once in Washington, Cox met with President Herbert Hoover. According to Rice, Cox "was a Republican, albeit a stormy and rebellious one."[103] In practical politics, though, Cox was unskilled. He switched parties from Republican to Democrat and back again, formed his own Jobless Party, and variously ran for president and called for the creation of a dictatorship.[104] Always his driving force seems to have been not his own promotion, but help for suffering people. In retrospect a religious historian seems safest seeing Cox's public antics as one priest being a fool for Christ, knowing that what seems foolish to secular eyes is wise before God.

Like truth, justice is neither liberal nor conservative, and as a priest Cox fed the hungry and defended the defenseless. It was the era of Pope Pius XI, a research librarian whose family had owned a silk mill. In 1931 the pope issued an encyclical letter, *Quadragesimo Anno,* marking the fortieth anniversary of Leo XIII's encyclical, *Rerum Novarum.* Pius XI restated Leo's concerns about just co-operation between the one who is hired and the one who hires, and he reminded people of their responsibility to be their brother's keepers, even to the point of using the state to protect the most vulnerable. Nevertheless, he emphasized the incompatibility of socialism, with its concomitant police state, and the Catholic belief in individual free will (*Quadragesimo Anno,* 119-131).[105] Cox drew inspiration and vindication from these social encyclicals, and he rooted his good works in prayer. All the while Cox was finding creative ways to help the poor, he was also serving as pastor of a city parish. His liturgical life as a priest deepened his devotion to Our Lady of Lourdes, and he led pilgrimages to Lourdes.

So much of what a priest does, though, goes unseen or unrecorded. He touches lives of people he has never met, in ways he never knows and by means of which he is often unaware. Rice noted that Cox is little remembered because "he left no paper trail."[106] Cox was a preacher and pastor; he was active and creative, but not a writer.

THE STAINED GLASS WINDOW

SERMONETTE BY REV. JAMES R. COX

ILLUSTRATED BY VIC PAUL

All the more fitting, then, that homilies Father Cox once sent over the ether waves of what was once called the wireless should have survived for historical study.

Cox was a priest of the diocese of Pittsburgh, and beginning in March, 1924, he delivered brief sermons on one of the city's radio stations, WJAS. Rice recalled that "Jimmy Cox…was made for radio, with his pleasant, flexible voice and his ease."[107] Around 1930 an artist named Victor Paul used these sermons as the basis for fifty-five pen and ink cartoons. When published in book form, they were called *Illustrated Lectures,* being further described as "fifteen minute sermons cut down to one minute."[108] Each cartoon has three frames, and the effect of Paul's black and white pictures combined with Cox's concise words calls to mind the once popular verses on signs alongside the road advertising Burma Shave. Since the book of cartoons has no pagination, it will be necessary to refer to the cartoons by number. They give us entertaining evidence of one priest's efforts to reach more and more people.

In the sixth in the series of cartoons, for example, the subject is education. "The little chick dies when not given proper care," reads the first frame, the picture showing a peep and a broken shell. The second shows two men dwarfed by the stark interior of a vast factory and adds, "Many a mill-hand would be an important engineer—had he the opportunity to pursue higher education." The final frame depicts a legendary inventor and concludes, "Many embryo Edisons are killed off educationally because of our negligence to provide for them higher educational opportunities." The idea and the images would have struck a chord with most people. In the 1920s not only poultry farmers kept chickens, and the care a mother hen gives her brood was familiar also from the Gospel. Immigrants, most of whom were Catholic, working in Pittsburgh's steel mills saw the need for their children to go to school and in some cases sent their sons to places like Saint Vincent. Both the dreaming schoolboy and the captain of industry could recognize the importance of nurturing the next Thomas Edison, by the 1920s a figure on par in the popular pantheon with Benjamin Franklin.

In the sixteenth cartoon, the moral is about tact and charity. It was the age of the League of Nations, when statesmen hoped that treaties would prevent wars. "Diplomacy," begins the first frame, a scene with men in suits deliberating around a table, "is important, not only in international relations, but should be applied in everyday life." The next frame shows a couple embracing and says, "Love and happiness is found in homes where both wife and husband use diplomacy in their relations with one another, in-laws, and neighbors." Lastly, we are shown a young man standing before an executive who sits behind a large desk. We are told that, "An employee is more sure of getting that raise if he is diplomatic; serious misunderstandings and hard feeling can often be avoided by use of diplomacy." Clearly, this message was not an incendiary call for workers to unite and lose nothing but their chains.

The thirtieth cartoon, using three familiar faces, appeals to American patriotism and Christian sentimentality. "Washington, whose culture, determination, and idealism," it begins, "gave us America, prayed to God for guidance during the crucial period of the struggle for independence." Then, using another image familiar from every schoolroom, Cox and Paul continue the theme. "Lincoln, to whose unflinching character we owe the unity of our nation, during the dark days of the Civil War often had talks with the Maker." Lest the point be lost, the last frame tells us, "Christ taught us when in need to turn in full confidence to God."

To choose a fourth and final sample, the forty-eighth cartoon sermon conveys what could be called Benedictine balance. "Some interpret life," says the first frame, "as a continuous grind." The picture is of a student bent over his desk, a glowing lamp showing he is studying late into the night. In that era of flappers and speakeasys, the next frame shows young couples dancing and says, "Others try to spend it seeking pleasures." The final frame shows the British House of Parliament and Big Ben in the moonlight. "There is a time for everything," the moral reads, "for work, sleep, praying, eating, and playing." The point is clear. "You will find life more pleasant if you do not overdo any one certain thing." The monks who had taught Cox theology would have been pleased.

Benedictine Seminarians in the Clerics' Garden ca. 1926

JUSTIN KRELLNER

During the 1930s and 1940s a model of monastic balance was Father Justin Krellner, O. S. B. Born in 1905 in the town of St. Marys, Pennsylvania, Roman Krellner attended rural and parochial schools in his native Elk County, and in 1925 he entered the monastic community of Saint Vincent. With his monastic habit he received the name Justin. He is remembered as an approachable man, simple in his way of life. Of medium height and thin of build, he was never robust. When he was at Sant' Anselmo, from 1929 to 1933, he would remark that during the winters, he could not keep his feet warm. Even upon his return home, poor circulation would bother him.

Nevertheless, as a student in Rome, Krellner absorbed the Thomism of Father Joseph Gredt, O. S. B., a native of Luxembourg and a monk of the abbey in Seckau, Austria. Gredt was nearing seventy and had an uncanny command of the *Summa Theologiae* and its commentaries, particularly those by Cajetan.[109] In June, 1931, Krellner was ordained priest by the vicar general of Pope Pius XI, and two years later, taking all of six weeks to write his dissertation, he completed his doctorate in sacred theology.

At Saint Vincent, Krellner taught Scripture. In the College he taught an introductory course on both old and new Testaments, and in the Seminary he taught exegesis. He had not specialized in Scripture, and he always described himself as a theologian who was self-taught in Scripture. He joined the Catholic Biblical Association and attended its meetings, keeping abreast of the Church's use of the historical-critical method. He taught by lecture, but with energy and enthusiasm still impressed upon the memories of his students. Krellner is remembered

Rev. Justin Krellner, O.S.B., in Rome

lecturing while gazing into some distant point in the room, as though he were mesmerized by an apparition. When touching upon a more mysterious passage of Scripture, he would smile and raise his right index finger and say, "Ah, we shall find the answer to that in Heaven!" Krellner's exams were short answer; he was more concerned with seeing whether the student could summarize the main points, not simply repeat what had been said in class.

In 1939, Krellner and his confrere, Father John Ujlaki, O. S. B., were approached by the Catholic Biblical Association to help with a new translation of the Bible.[110] They agreed to translate II Samuel, the result of their work eventually appearing in what is now known as the New American Bible. Ujlaki was a monastic character, irascible and gruff. He had been a monk of Saint Martin's, in Pannonhalma, Hungary, and he had known of Saint Vincent through his studies at Sant' Anselmo. Students called him "Hungry John," a reference not only to his nationality, but also to his beefy frame; a jowly man fond of cigars, Ujlaki was a stark contrast to the quiet and ascetic Krellner. Ujlaki was a linguist, and he taught Hebrew and Greek. Former students of Ujlaki recall his frequent warning, "I flunk you till you pass!"

Krellner's friends included Patrick Cummins, a monk and priest of Conception Abbey, in northwestern Missouri. Cummins, twenty-five years Krellner's senior, was a colleague in the Catholic Biblical Association. Both men had studied in Rome, Cummins returning in the early 1920s to serve as rector of Sant' Anselmo. Back in America, he published an English translation of Dante's *Divina Commedia*, calling it *Dante, Theologian.* Cummins and Krellner shared an interest in Thomistic philosophy as well as Scripture, and Dante bridged these two fields. "For all his learning," someone once said of Cummins, "he was as simple as the most unlearned lay brother," and he "delighted in carrying on long conversations with the lay brothers of the monastery."[111] This simplicity marked Krellner as well, who was seemingly as happy repairing watches or working in his rose garden as he was in a classroom lecturing on the Bible.

In July, 1949, at age forty-four, Krellner died suddenly of a heart attack while vacationing with his brother; Krellner had just said Mass and had gone upstairs to shave. Cummins remembered his friend, saying Krellner was "very regular in all his duties, particularly attendance at choir," and through this "life…of a genuine monk," he "communicated his own spirit to younger men."[112] The day after Krellner's death, Archabbot Alfred Koch received word from the abbot primate, Bernard Kälin, that he wanted to name Krellner the new rector of Sant' Anselmo.[113] Had he lived, Krellner would thus have followed in the footsteps of his old friend, Cummins. These unassuming monks brought to their monasteries and schools the splendor of the truth they had found in the Eternal City. "Sant' Anselmo," recalled one of Krellner's students, "contributed much to the theological, philosophical, and intellectual life of the seminary and the monastery at Latrobe."[114]

SPEAKING IN TONGUES

While the Roman influence was noticeable, Saint Vincent was also a melting pot. German continued to be the dominant language and culture of the monastery, and English predominated in the College. In the Seminary, most classes were taught in Latin, using ecclesiastical pronunciation. Students learned Latin in the College from Father Michael Hlavcak, O.S.B.,

Rev. John Ujlaki, O.S.B. (left) and Archabbot Alfred Koch, O.S.B.

who had edited Lorenz Englmann's *Latin Grammar*. Hlavcak was
a native Slovak, part of a grow-
ing minority at the monastery.
To meet the pastoral needs of a
large constituency of immigrants,
the Seminary offered courses in
the Slovak language. Father Hubert Macko, O. S. B., himself an
ethnic Slovak, taught the language, and in 1926 he published
a grammar book for students of
Slovak.[115]

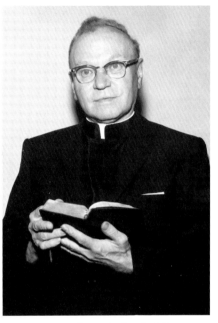

As Slovaks and other eth-
nic groups sought to become assimilated into American culture,
the need for seminarians to learn
Slovak decreased. Nevertheless,
with cultural assimilation poten-

Rev. Hubert Macko, O.S.B.

tial priests and priests themselves faced new challenges. The pre-
vailing ethos of America in the twentieth century was that of Eng-
lish-speaking Protestants who were content to be what Napoleon
contemptuously called England, a nation of shopkeepers. In such an
environment, priests needed practical training, and in the Seminary
they had a course in the (for some) abstruse language of mathematics. The basis for it was a textbook written by Saint Vincent's Father Daniel Kaib, *Bookkeeping for Parish Priests*, in print from 1910
to 1932. While learning how to balance the parish books, Catholic priests faced the problem of their flocks drifting away from the
Catholic faith as they blended in speech and manners with their
Protestant neighbors and co-workers.

SECOND WORLD WAR

One factor in the integration of Catholics into the mainstream of American culture was the Second World War. Although the Church had reached a chilly truce with Benito Mussolini, his invasion of Abyssinia (modern Ethiopia) gave nations of the North Atlantic pause. At the same time, a militant combination of nationalism and socialism in Germany presented what Winston Churchill was to call "a gathering storm." In September, 1939, Germany invaded Poland, striking the spark that ignited the war in Europe.

In December, 1941, the Japanese surprise attack on Pearl Harbor jolted America from her complacent isolation, however cozy an ideal, and it shook Catholics from their enclaves, called by some scholars "Catholic ghettoes." As with so many cultural phenomena of the period, this cracking open of so-called ghettoes was not unique to Catholics. For example, since the late seventeenth century, in Pennsylvania alone members of certain sects of German Protestants tended to settle together, speaking their ancestral Swiss-German dialects among themselves until after the Second World War.

The effect of that war on the Seminary was threefold. First, enrollment declined, young men delaying the pursuit of their priestly vocations in order to serve in the armed forces. Second, diocesan students who would have gone to Rome were sent to Saint Vincent. Third, monks of Saint Vincent who would otherwise have been sent to Rome for studies were instead sent to the Pontifical Institute of Mediaeval Studies in Toronto. These monks were Roderick Baronner, Germain Lieb, and Eric McCormick.[116] The recollection of one of these men is that Archabbot Alfred Koch summoned them to his office, told them he was sending them to Toronto, and said, "And don't all study the same thing!"

From 1939 to 1946, Monsignor Gerald Phelan was president of

the Pontifical Institute, founded in 1929 by Etienne Gilson. Phelan, an astute administrator and avid Thomist, described the program at the Pontifical Institute. "The aim of all instruction at the" Institute, Phelan explained, "is to provide its students with a rigidly scientific training in study and research."[117] This scientific instruction assumed fluency in Latin and emphasized what Phelan called "practical work in palaeography,"[118] although men who anticipated work in parishes were less sure of its practicality. While learning how to interpret medieval manuscripts, students also became steeped in Scholastic thought. With these foundations, a student could then specialize in a particular aspect of medieval civilization. This rigorous intellectual environment was meant to make the students bridge-builders between the history and the future of the Church.

LIFE AFTER SEMINARY

Once a man had finished his studies in the Seminary, if his bishop or abbot deemed him worthy, he received holy orders. The normal course of orders was subdeacon, deacon, and then priest. Whether ordained for a diocese or as a member of a monastery, the new priests were expected to keep current with developments in the subjects they had studied in seminary. To encourage them to stay abreast of Church teaching, the Seminary employed something called Quinquennials.

For five years after ordination, priests educated at the Seminary were required to return once a year for oral examinations. Most dioceses had their own review boards, but some had their men go back to the Seminary for grilling. Monks of Saint Vincent who had been ordained to the priesthood certainly had to return to their alma mater. The young priests sat in the corridor of Leander Hall and waited to be called in to the parlor. There behind a long table sat the rector, the archabbot, and two professors. For an hour they asked questions in Latin, and the young priest fielded them as best he could with the Latin he remembered. Questions ranged across the various facets of dogmatic and moral theology, for example, one year perhaps focusing primarily on the Trinity, another year on grace.

DEMOGRAPHICS

Jerome Oetgen has called the 1920s "in many ways…a golden age for Saint Vincent Seminary."[119] Seminarians came from various dioceses in Pennsylvania and Ohio, including Cleveland, Harrisburg, Pittsburgh, and Toledo. Until the early 1970s, monks followed a pattern worn smooth with long use. From farms and coal patches in western Pennsylvania, Catholic families, chiefly German, Irish, and Slovak, sent to Saint Vincent boys in their early teens.

These boys entered the Scholasticate of Saint Vincent. This school, based on a European model, consisted of six years of minor seminary, being four years of high school and two years of college. In the Scholasticate, students led a life steeped in Latin, Greek, spiritual reading, and athletics. Upon completing the sophomore year in the College, a scholastic entered the monastery's novitiate for a year and then returned to college to complete his bachelor's degree in philosophy. After receiving his degree in philosophy, he began his studies in theology, culminating in ordination to the priesthood.

By 1971, Saint Vincent had closed the Scholasticate, a response to a trend of the times when enrollment in seminaries and memberships in monastic communities declined. Saint Vincent Seminary fared better than most, with dioceses such as Pittsburgh and Harrisburg continuing to have confidence in its ability to train young men for the priesthood. Saint Vincent continued to teach Latin and Aquinas and other essential aspects of theology, thus giving men a solid grounding; how each man chose to build upon that foundation stands outside the scope of this book. The late 1960s and early 1970s saw a development of the student population of our Seminary, with admission being open to lay students and religious sisters. Moreover, with the admission of non-clerical monks to solemn vows with full chapter rights as choir monks, college and seminary education became open to monks who were not seeking ordination. This happier field of the expansion of seminary education will be surveyed next.

4

WELCOME RENEWAL
OF THE WHOLE CHURCH

For young people of the early twenty-first century, America in the 1950s seems remote both in time and in importance. For those young people, the 1950s seem as antique as Johnstown before the flood, an age of innocence before a disaster, in this case the social and political upheaval of the 1960s and the stagnation and bad taste

Pope Pius XII

of the 1970s. Fifty-odd years ago the grave threat to the morals of American youth was Buddy Holly; he made the raucous Swing music of the previous two decades seem as genteel as a symphony by Joseph Haydn. Framed in formal portraits to preside over this mythical 1950s, combining as it does nostalgia and condescension, are two old men who have not fared well with academicians, Dwight Eisenhower and Pius XII. The retired general and the reclusive pon-

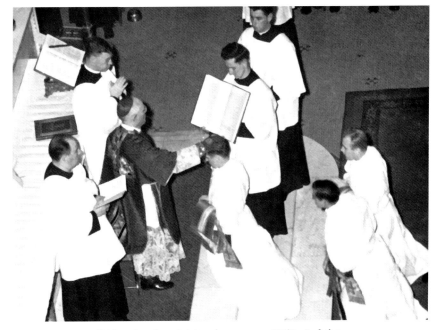

*Bishop Lamb ordaining deacons ca. 1953. At left is
Rev. Oliver A. Grosselin, O.S.B., Rector.*

tiff seemed to stand for an era remembered, when it is recalled at
all, for stuffy paternalism. To paraphrase Galileo, yet still there was
movement.

Students of history see in the 1950s a confluence of ideas excit-
ing debate within the Church since at least the early years of the
twentieth century. Just as Eisenhower could not have built America's interstate highway system without the automobile, so too, Pius
XII could not have instituted changes in the Roman liturgy without what has been called the liturgical movement. The automobile
provided people with more efficient mobility, and the reform of the
liturgy brought the lay faithful to focus more keenly upon the altar
and the once-for-all sacrifice of Christ on the Cross.

While the parallel may seem at first far-fetched, the point remains that the general trend of the twentieth century, at least in

Europe and the European diaspora, was one of individuals covering vast distances quickly, all in search of a better life. Within the sphere of man's religious life, Catholics were seeing their liturgy returned to earlier sources in order to help believers in their quest for holiness, their eternal union with God. The liturgical movement sought to use art, architecture, and music to encourage people to see the Mass as the central aspect of their lives as Christians. At the beginning of the century, Pius X promoted the use of Gregorian chant and the frequent reception of Communion; by the middle of the century, Pius XII placed renewed emphasis upon the Paschal mystery by restoring the Easter Vigil, during the patristic and medieval centuries the most important time of the Christian year.

When Pius XII died, an austere octogenarian with congestive heart failure, his jolly and rotund successor, John XXIII, seemed a striking contrast. Pius XII came from an aristocratic family of Rome,

Diocesan seminarians at Benediction in the Basilica, ca. 1958 with Rev. Oliver A. Grosselin, O.S.B., Rector, presiding.

Pope John XXIII

while John XXIII grew up on a small farm in the hills of northern Italy. Yet both men had sharp minds and the gift of administration, serving the Church as Vatican diplomats and authors of graceful prose. Both men encouraged the reform of the sacred liturgy, the liturgical movement fostered by Benedictines in the early twentieth century having impressed both pontiffs.

In 1962, John XXIII sought to strengthen what he saw as lax educational standards for Catholic seminaries. He did so by issuing an Apostolic Constitution encouraging the study of Latin. He emphasized the need for bishops and religious superiors to ensure theological instruction be conducted in Latin, since Latin is like a doorway into the world of Christian writers of the past, thus binding together the generations (*Veterum Sapientiae* 8).[120] As a bishop of Pittsburgh observed, John XXIII believed priests could better minister in the people's native tongue if as seminarians they had learned the historic language of the Church. "There was nothing whatsoever inconsistent," wrote John Wright, "about his pastoral option for the vernacular liturgy and his cultural determination to preserve Latin studies,"[121] both for the liberal arts and for theology.

Other learned men were concerned over Catholic education. One such was Christopher Dawson, an English convert to Catholicism and eminent historian. In 1914 Dawson had entered the Church after growing up in the Anglican tradition, and for the next forty years he made a name for himself as a scholar of Christian humanism. In 1958 he began teaching at Harvard, becoming its first

Charles Chauncey Stillman Professor of Roman Catholic Studies.

Dawson was a product of an Anglican university, Oxford, and was a professor at one founded by Puritans, Harvard, and as a Catholic layman he gave much thought to Catholic higher education. "[M]aterial institutional growth has outstripped spiritual creativeness,"[122] he observed. The emphasis by prelates upon "bricks and mortar" and upon cultural assimilation by immigrants contributed to this trend. "But in so far as this is true," Dawson conceded, "the fault lies with our civilization as a whole," so that "higher education inevitably answers the demands of the society which it serves."[123] He foresaw the possibility of Catholic colleges and universities becoming more accommodating to the secular culture.

Since seminarians come from the same secular environment as more conventional graduate students, this compromise with secularism would have an effect on seminaries as well. Dawson saw one worthwhile solution. "It is necessary," he said, "to extend the range of modern education not so much in width as in depth," and according to him, "the obvious way to do this is by a better understanding of the Christian tradition as *the spiritual source and the moral basis of our culture.*"[124] This renewed interest by leading Catholic intellectuals in

Ordination Class of 1960

the wisdom of the ancients and the faith of the Fathers, inspired in the midst of splendid liturgical celebrations, became the charismatic prelude to the spiritual phenomenon of the Second Vatican Council. That council's importance to Catholic seminaries requires us to take a further look at it.

SECOND VATICAN COUNCIL

In late January, 1959, Pope John XXIII visited the Benedictine abbey of Saint Paul's Outside the Walls in Rome, and there told a group of seventeen cardinals about his plan to call an ecumenical council. Since the Vatican Council of 1869-1870 had never formally adjourned, John XXIII decided to reconvene the Vatican Council. On 11 October, 1962, John XXIII opened the first session of the Council; in 1965, Paul VI closed the Second Vatican Council. In June, 1963, John XXIII had lost his struggle with cancer, and the college of cardinals met in conclave in the Sistine Chapel to elect his

Archabbot Denis Strittmatter, O.S.B.

successor. They chose the cardinal archbishop of Milan, Giovanni Battista Montini, who as pope took the name Paul VI.

During those four years between 1962 and 1965, some two thousand prelates from around the world, including Saint Vincent's retired archabbot, Denis Strittmatter, met at the Vatican for the four sessions of the Council. As had Boniface Wimmer at Vatican I, Archabbot Denis attended the Council as Abbot President of the American Cassinese Congregation. Among the bishops participating in the Council were Fulton J. Sheen, noted for his popular television show and scores of books, and Karol Wojtyla, who would in 1978 become Pope John Paul II. The causes for canonization of both men are now open before the Holy See. During the Council Pope Paul VI took time to meet with the Orthodox patriarch, Athenagoras, in Jerusalem, the first meeting between pope and patriarch for nearly a thousand years. As at the Council of Trent, Protestant observers, such as Lutheran scholar George A. Lindbeck, were present.[125] Behind the scenes were Catholic theologians, such as Joseph Ratzinger, now Pope Benedict XVI, to advise the bishops.

In the years following the Council, theologians and the laity discussed at length the Council's sixteen documents. From 1978 to 2005 a father of the Council, John Paul II, preached and wrote on all aspects of the Council. Thus, for the first time since Leo XIII, there was an opportunity for the Church to have conciliar documents explained and implemented by a bishop who had played a significant part in their drafting.

Most significant for the history of Saint Vincent Seminary is the Council's decree on the education of priests, *Optatam totius*, promulgated by Pope Paul VI on 28 October, 1965. The title comes from the first two words of the opening sentence, which one can translate, "Welcome renewal of the whole Church."[126] The decree continues to say that this welcome renewal depends upon the proper formation of priests, and it adds that their formation must be animated by the spirit of Christ. In March, 1992, after a synod of bishops, John Paul II issued an Apostolic Exhortation, *Pastores dabo vobis* ("I will give you shepherds"), discussing among other aspects of the priesthood the educational ideals set forth in *Optatam totius*. To these texts we now turn.

Section Five of *Optatam totius* addresses seminary education. According to this document, seminarians, after training in ancient, mediaeval, and modern philosophy, should be taught Scripture and the Fathers of the Church. Canon law and salvation history must also have their places, and "in order to throw as full a light as possible on the mysteries of salvation," seminarians should take as their guide Saint Thomas Aquinas (*Optatam totius*, 16). Uniting all these studies should be the liturgy, "the first and indispensable source of the true Christian spirit" (*Optatam totius,* 16). The Fathers of the Council emphasize the need for bishops to select men of virtue, so that their academic and liturgical formation should prepare the seminarian to embrace his pastoral duties as a priest. The seminary should thus be ready to form the seminarians' minds and hearts, intellectual and prayer lives flowing together to bring forth works of charity.

When commenting in 1992 on this decree of the Council, Pope John Paul II focused on four points. He noted that the decree speaks of the formation of seminarians being human, spiritual, intellectual, and pastoral. He discusses the need for maturity and balance, especially when accepting fully the gift of celibacy, and thus the priest's special espousal to the Church. The pope cites Thomas Aquinas to support his point that "the whole of theology is ordered to nourishing the faith" (*Pastores dabo vobis* 53). He further relies on Aquinas to underscore that when studying theology, study done with prayer, the seminarians must see the discourse among theologians co-operating with the living tradition of the Church, the magisterium of Peter. These aspects of formation, the pope concluded, when combined with a desire to become what *Optatam totius* called a "shepherd of souls" (*Pastores dabo vobis* 57), would provide the Church with worthy priests. An integrated sense of manhood, informed by Scripture and prayer, buttressed by philosophy and the magisterial tradition of the Church, will help form priests who will yearn to preach the Good News.

AQUINAS AND WIMMER HALLS

Aquinas Hall

At Saint Vincent, the setting for this course of study and formation was a pair of buildings new since the Second World War.[127] Since the First World War, burgeoning enrollment convinced the Seminary that it would soon outgrow its new hall. Pressure for living space came also from increased enrollment in the College, the G. I. Bill making college education affordable to veterans. In 1950 the Seminary broke ground for a residence hall and a building with classrooms; these buildings joined at right angles and formed a quadrangle with the monastic library and Anselm Hall. In August, 1952, the abbot primate of the Benedictine Order, Bernard Kälin, travelled from Rome and blessed the new seminary buildings.

The new dormitory was named Wimmer Hall, the new academic wing, Aquinas Hall. Aquinas was three stories, Wimmer six. Both buildings were red brick, matching the other structures on campus, with gabled roofs of slate and window frames painted white. Inside, floors were tile, and steam radiators heated the rooms. Above the main door to Wimmer Hall was a verse from Psalm 34, *Venite, filii, audite me, timorem Domini docebo vos,* "Come, my sons, listen to me, and I shall teach you the fear of the Lord." This text was chosen not only because it features prominently in

Wimmer Hall

95

the Prologue to the Holy Rule of Saint Benedict, but also and more significantly, because it begins Saint Ambrose's *De Officiis Ministrorum*, his manual for training priests in their duties.

Some seminarians who moved into Wimmer Hall were veterans of the war. A battle-hardened student body required a realistic approach to policies and procedures. "When I was in charge of discipline in our seminary," recalled a former rector, "I soon learned not to see and hear everything."[128] Nevertheless, spartan conformity prevailed, something not unknown to military veterans.

The Seminary catalogue for 1954, the first to be printed in English instead of Latin, makes clear the rules, virtually unchanged in thirty or forty years. On campus, seminarians were required to wear a cassock and a Roman collar, with black trousers, socks, and shoes beneath. Seminarians also needed to supply their own biretta and two white surplices. Off campus, seminarians wore black clerical suits, black hats, and overcoats. Photographs of the period show the hats in the fedora style. When away from the Seminary, seminarians who had received holy orders, such as diaconate, wore Roman collars, while others wore white dress shirts and black neckties. Rooms came furnished and provided with sheets; seminarians were to bring their own blankets and towels. Also, the only piece of furniture they could bring was a typewriter stand.

NEW LIBRARY

These new seminary buildings enjoyed proximity to the library for six years. Since its construction in 1892, the library had been below the choir chapel, an easy walk indoors from Aquinas Hall. On the ceiling of the library were paintings to guide the student to the section he sought. For example, the stacks containing books on the Gospel were beneath paintings of the four Evangelists; books by and

Aerial view of campus before the fire of 1963

Interior of the old Library

The new Library under construction

Aerial of campus after the fire of January 28, 1963

about the Church Fathers were beneath paintings of the four Doctors of the Western Church.

In 1956 ground was broken on a slope just west of the Preparatory School for a new library, designed to hold the hitherto disparate libraries of the Prep School, the College, and the Archabbey.[129] Seminarians used the archabbey library, and with the new library building, the old archabbey library became the monastic refectory. In April, 1958, the new library building, holding three distinct libraries, was dedicated. Francis Cardinal Spellman of New York blessed the building, and Anselm Albareda, O. S. B., a monk of Montserrat in Spain and prefect of the Vatican Library, delivered an address on Benedictine libraries, his heavy Spanish accent distracting some of the audience.[130]

FIRE AND ICE

In January, 1963, fire swept through the buildings of Saint Vincent.[131] The red brick structures, with floors supported by beams of chestnut wood, were connected one to the other; fire ravaged the monastic quadrangle. Many of the buildings were a hundred years old, the timber frames dry as kindling. Water from fire hoses froze almost as soon as it hit the walls of the buildings; as much damage was done by water and ice as well as by fire and smoke. Buildings not gutted by flames were buckled by freezing water.

Fire fighters kept the blaze from reaching several buildings, including the basilica, Leander Hall, Maur Hall, and Aquinas and Wimmer Halls. The new library, unconnected to the other buildings, was untouched. The Seminary lost one week of school, but in addition to ruined buildings, the fire left scars on the memory of the community. With the changes necessitated by the destruction from the fire occurring around the same time as the changes introduced by the Second Vatican Council, life at Saint Vincent was never the same.

DEMETRIUS DUMM

The rector who steered the Seminary through the choppy waves rippling out from the Council was Father Demetrius Dumm, O. S. B. Robert Dumm was born in 1923 into a large farming family of German descent; the farm was on rolling hills north of Carrolltown. In 1940 he was graduated from the prep school at Saint Vincent, and in 1942 he entered the novitiate of the Archabbey. There he was given the name Demetrius, in honor of the pioneer Catholic missionary of Pennsylvania, Demetrius Gallitzin. In due course Demetrius Dumm made his solemn vows and in 1943 began his theological studies at the Seminary. He admits to envying his confreres who were sent to study at the Pontifical Institute of Mediaeval Studies in Toronto, and he secretly longed to join them.

Rev. Demetrius R. Dumm, O.S.B.

In 1946, Archabbot Alfred Koch sent Dumm to study at Sant' Anselmo. With the end of the War, it was safe to send monks to Rome for schooling. At Sant' Anselmo he studied under Cipriano Vagaggini, O. S. B., a monk from Belgium. Vagaggini suggested that Dumm combine his interest in Scripture with his monastic calling and so delve into the writings of Saint Jerome, monk and biblical scholar. In the summers Dumm would go to the abbey at Metten, and there he wrote his dissertation.

While studying in Rome, Dumm became eligible to receive holy orders. Since Dumm could not sail home in time to be ordained with his classmates, Archabbot Alfred sent Dumm dimissorial letters and told him to find a bishop who would ordain him. In 1947 at the monastery at Subiaco, he was ordained to the priesthood; the ordaining bishop was Lorenzo Salvi, O. S. B., who was also abbot of Subiaco. Three years later, Dumm completed his Doctorate of Sacred Theology, but more school was in store. From Rome he was sent to Jerusalem to study Scripture at the Ecole Biblique. There he studied under two famous French Dominicans, Pierre Benoit, one of the translators of the French edition of the Jerusalem Bible, and Roland de Vaux, excavator of Qumran. It was a turbulent time, Israel having just won its independence after decades of the British Mandate.

Dumm was studying in Rome when Justin Krellner died, and Dumm worried that he would be called home before finishing his degree. His worries faded when word came from the archabbot not only to stay and finish the degree, but also to pursue a licence in Sacred Scripture at the Ecole Biblique. He finished the licence in 1952 and returned to Rome for two weeks of exams, given only at the Vatican. Upon returning to Saint Vincent, though, Dumm found himself teaching all the courses in Scripture. He also taught Greek and Hebrew.

To teach all these classes he set up a three-year cycle, covering the Synoptic Gospels, the Fourth Gospel, and the Epistles of Saint Paul; as was the custom then, in one lecture hall gathered the seminarians in second, third, and fourth theology, some seventy students in all. Although his first year Dumm made the mistake of assigning a research paper, taking him weeks to grade, he settled into a pattern of giving three essay exams per semester. "It was providential," he later said, "that I was forced to study all parts of the Scripture, because I was able to see the larger context."[132] As other Benedictines completed their studies and joined the faculty, Dumm was able to concentrate his teaching on the New Testament.

In addition to teaching, Dumm helped at local parishes, although he tended to be sent to All Saints in Masontown, a small town in the southwestern corner of Pennsylvania. He thus gained pastoral experience, often among rural people much like the ones he knew growing up. In 1955 he became vice rector of the Seminary, a position he held until 1963, when he was appointed rector. It was another turbulent time, with Saint Vincent just emerging from its devastating fire and the Church at large facing the heady days of the Second Vatican Council.

In an era when other seminaries were closing or becoming "houses of studies," Saint Vincent kept true to its mission of priestly formation. During the four years of the Council, its deliberations were secret; the debates and the documents of the Council were in Latin. As the decrees of the Council became public, their implementation was open to various readings. Rectors such as Dumm were faced with the often lapidary, but not always precise, prose composed by Vatican scribes. "We were flying by the seat of our pants," he told me. Necessity being the mother of invention, Dumm devised innovative solutions.

Above all, Dumm realized, a seminary must be a pastoral school, not a graduate school. Bishops and abbots sent their men to seminaries to learn how to be priests. "The seminarians," Dumm told me, "needed to know how to use knowledge, not how to write a new book." Dumm enlisted the help of his faculty, asking them to take on administrative roles such as academic dean and dean of students. Previously, there had been no deans, only a vice rector. Dumm attributed the collegiality of his faculty to their common Benedictine formation. Moreover, the monks lived and ate and prayed together, whereas diocesan seminaries, he recalls, tended to have their professors living apart and alone.

To prepare the seminarians in his charge to become leaders in the Church, Dumm saw that new rules were in order. Seminarians in the middle and later 1960s tended to be older than in previous decades, and Dumm recognized their maturity. He borrowed an idea from the military and began peer evaluations. Seminarians were asked to fill out a form to evaluate their fellow seminarians; one of the questions asked whether the seminarian could see the other student in question as the seminarian's own pastor. Meanwhile, Dumm replaced the old rule book with weekly conferences and written directives. He said that the rules were important, but more important was learning the theological reason behind them. Law without charity, order without reason, failed to integrate the inner and the outer man. "We knew we had to raise the fence and move it," Dumm told me, "but we weren't sure where to set it back down, and we met with some resistance."

Seminarians resisted the new regime in two ways. One was to argue for the old way, comfort being in the known. Some seemed to find freedom in unreflective obedience. Another was to invoke the spirit of the times, a restless spirit of defiance and self-indulgence. Some students insisted that eligibility for ordination should be put to a vote of the seminarians. Dumm rejected this congregationalist ecclesiology and gave conferences on the dangers of the avant garde. The offended seminarians sought solace from a monk who taught sociology in the College (whose name I know but do not record), a man given to progressive critiques and who later became a leading Mormon. He called Dumm "that Torquemada," referring to the fifteenth-century Dominican best known for his part in the Spanish Inquisition.

During this time, Dumm himself kept teaching, leading by example. To give seminarians different angles on theology, Dumm hit upon a labor-intensive but effective approach. With courses such as Christology or Sacraments, he led team teaching. Five professors would take turns lecturing, each present to hear the others' lectures. Dumm presented the Scriptural basis, while others in turn addressed the subject in terms of the Fathers of the Church, Saint Thomas Aquinas, or such modern authors as Edward Schillebeeckx. Students were required to write summaries of each lecture, and on Fridays the five professors fielded questions from the class. Meanwhile, students had their usual courses in canon law, exegesis, and Church history taught by one professor each.

Dumm had an engaging presence in the classroom. He was animated and witty, and he readily acknowledged his debt to his beloved professor, Justin Krellner. Dumm was often in demand as a retreat master, speaking to religious communities and dioceses around the country and abroad. His travels as a retreat master have taken him from England to Taiwan, Mexico to Ireland. From 1980 to 1983 he served his monastic community as master of novices, and each spring after this term of service he taught the novices a class on the spirituality of the Bible. He is warmly remembered for his avuncular manner in making the Scriptures pertinent to men beginning their monastic journeys.

In the midst of the busy round of administration and teaching, Dumm made time to write. He has said that as a student, "I dreamed of going into my monastic cell and studying tomes and writing learned articles."[133] He had finished his doctoral dissertation in 1950, but not until 1961 did he have a chance to publish it, a slim yet erudite study on *The Theological Basis of Virginity According to Saint Jerome*. Dumm contributed articles to *The American Benedictine Review* and *Worship*, and in 1980 he wrote a sixteen-page pamphlet for the United States Conference of Catholic Bishops, *The Bible and Respect for Life*. He also contributed entries to works of reference, notably the *Collegeville Pastoral Dictionary of Biblical Theology* and both editions of *The Jerome Bible Commentary*.

In 1987 Dumm published his first book on spirituality, *Flowers in the Desert: A Spirituality of the Bible*, and it has gone through three printings. Since then he has written four other books, all on some aspect of Scripture: *Cherish Christ Above All* (1996) discusses the use of the Bible in the Holy Rule of Saint Benedict; *A Mystical Portrait of Jesus* (2001) is a meditative study of the Gospel of John; *Praying the Scriptures* (2003) revisits themes found in *Flowers in the Desert* and expands upon them, including musings on the Rosary. Most recently, he has published *So We Do Not Lose Heart*, a collection of eighty-three reflections on passages of Scripture dealing in one way or another with aging. In each book he brings together his training in the historical-critical method and his practice of *lectio divina*, the prayerful reading of Scripture. Dumm's books are marked by a clear and brisk style, and much like C. S. Lewis, he has a gift for finding apt examples from everyday life. Dumm attributes this ability to his life as a priest. "My pastoral work," he said, "helped me see the Bible as a guide for people's lives that helps us deal with the real problems of life."[134]

When Pope Paul VI passed away, in 1978, Dumm went to the archabbot, Egbert Donovan, and asked to be relieved of his post as rector. Dumm pointed out that he had begun his time as rector when Paul VI had been elected to the papal throne, so it only stood to reason that he should leave office upon the pope's death. Archabbot Egbert brushed aside this characteristically witty logic, and so Dumm served another two years.

Demetrius Dumm's successor as rector, Father John Haag, O.S.B., sought to build upon Dumm's legacy by taking steps to change the Seminary into a theological graduate school. For a few years in the early 1980s the Seminary's catalogue bore the name of "Saint Vincent Seminary/School of Theology." The idea seems to have been to make it a graduate school for any and all to study theology and spirituality. This notion found scant support, and the Seminary model stayed intact, its main purpose remaining its tried and true, yet ever adapting, program of priestly formation. The program's adaptation and continuation found capable hands in Benedictine Fathers Thomas Acklin and Kurt Belsole. Acklin had earned a doctorate from the Catholic University of Louvain in theology and also trained as a psychoanalyst. Belsole, a patristics scholar, had his doctorate from Sant' Anselmo, where he had taught one semester a year before becoming rector at Saint Vincent, serving until 2006, when Father Justin Matro was appointed. Matro, who earned his doctorate from the Gregorian Pontifical University in Rome, had been vice rector of the Seminary since 2003.[135]

As has been noted above, dioceses and religious communities have consistently entrusted their men to Saint Vincent Seminary. Currently, two archdioceses, thirteen dioceses and six religious communities send students to the Seminary. The archdioceses are:

Rev. Thomas Acklin, O.S.B.

Rev. Kurt Belsole, O.S.B.

Very Rev. Justin Matro, O.S.B.

Atlanta, Georgia and Campinas, Brazil. The dioceses are: Altoona-Johnstown; Charleston, South Carolina; Covington, Kentucky; Erie; Greensburg; Harrisburg; Ogdensburg, New York; Pittsburgh; Saint Thomas, Virgin Islands; Savannah, Georgia; Steubenville, Ohio; Wheeling-Charleston, West Virginia and Youngstown, Ohio. The religious communities are: Conception Abbey, Missouri; Sacred and Immaculate Hearts of Jesus and Mary, Ohio; Saint Benedict's Abbey, Atchison, Kansas; Saint Bernard Abbey, Cullman, Alabama; Subiaco Abbey, Arkansas and Saint Vincent Archabbey.

WILLIAM G. CONNARE

Along with Archabbot Denis Strittmatter, Saint Vincent Seminary had another alumnus at the Council. William G. Connare had been ordained in 1936, and in 1960 he was consecrated the second bishop of Greensburg. The Diocese of Greensburg had been created in 1951 from the diocese of Pittsburgh, the first bishop being Monsignor Hugh Lamb, a priest of the Archdiocese of Philadelphia.[136] Lamb had grown up in Coatesville, a small industrial city between Lancaster and Philadelphia, and he had studied for the priesthood at Saint Charles Seminary in Overbrook, Pennsylvania, before being sent to study at the North American College in Rome. In 1935 he became auxiliary bishop of Philadelphia, the position he held when he was named the first Bishop of Greensburg. Short and stocky, he had a reserve few could pierce. As a Philadelphian, he adapted to his new see in the Appalachian hills on his own terms, apparently like a Roman proconsul stationed in a distant province.

Unlike Lamb, Connare had been born in 1911 in Pittsburgh, and he was graduated from Duquesne University before entering Saint Vincent Seminary.[137] In 1934, he earned a Master's degree from Saint Vincent College, his thesis being "Is the Human Soul

Immortal?" In his early years as a priest, he worked in the city of Pittsburgh, holding various administrative posts, such as director of the diocesan Society for the Propagation of the Faith. In December, 1959, Bishop Lamb suffered a heart attack and died; in February the following year Pope John XXIII appointed Connare to succeed Lamb.

As a bishop, Connare was busy building up the Diocese of Greensburg.

Bishop William G. Connare

Greensburg, the county seat of Westmoreland County, is ten miles west of Saint Vincent, and the diocese has the monastery within its limits. He opened three schools, including Clelian Heights School for Exceptional Children, where children with learning disabilities found a home, with Apostles of the Sacred Heart staffing the school and providing strong emphasis on the faith. In 1961, Connare founded *The Catholic Accent*, a weekly newspaper for the diocese, and he wrote a regular column for it.

Connare's years of almost perpetual motion as bishop were nonetheless marked by prayer. He is remembered for his strong devotion to the Eucharist, as well as to the Blessed Mother. In December, 1961, Connare convened the first synod of the diocese, saying it "must quicken in our hearts an appreciation of our vocation to follow Christ in all things."[138] To prepare for the synod, he called upon the faithful to pray for it, saying, "This work will prosper only in a spirit of prayer."[139]

As Bishop of Greensburg, Connare attended all four sessions of the Second Vatican Council, in November, 1962, addressing it on the subject of the prayer of the Church, namely in the breviary and the Divine Office. He proposed that priests be given the option, when praying their breviary in private, to do so in the vernacular. While granting that "all priests should know Latin," Connare suggested that a priest's pastoral life would improve if he "could assimilate the sacred riches from the breviary in the same language in which he preaches to" the people of God "from the pulpit."[140] In 1967 Connare made his own pastoral role as a teacher clear; at a priestly ordination at Saint Vincent, with the abbey church full of lay people, Bishop Connare preached, a full year before *Humanae vitae*, on the Church's traditional teaching about artificial birth control.

In 1975 he was again in Rome, concelebrating at the Mass for the canonization of Elizabeth Ann Seton. Five years later he was in San Salvador for the funeral Mass of assassinated Archbishop Oscar Romero. During the funeral, gunfire rang out, and forty people were killed. "I remember wondering," Connare later said, "if our time had come."[141] Frightened but otherwise unharmed, Connare survived and returned to his diocese, there to serve until his retirement in 1987.

He passed away eight years later. At the Council one American observer had described Connare as one of the bishops who "spoke honestly and had a warm love for their people."[142] Connare is still recalled fondly as a model bishop, one who did not wear his erudition on his sleeve, dignified but not pompous. Upon Connare's death, Donald Wuerl, Bishop of Pittsburgh, said Connare "was a humble and holy man," who was "a good shepherd molded in the image of Christ."[143]

PAULINUS SELLE

A younger contemporary of Connare became a fixture at the Seminary for fifty-seven years. Father Paulinus J. Selle, O. S. B., was born in 1914 in St. Marys, Pennsylvania.[144] Baptised Jerome Selle, at age fourteen he entered the Scholasticate of Saint Vincent. In 1930

Rev. Paulinus Selle, O.S.B.

he entered the novitiate of the archabbey, receiving the monastic name of Paulinus. From 1936 to 1939 he studied at Sant' Anselmo, coming under the tutelage of Father Burkhard Neunheuser, a Benedictine from Baria Laach, a leading center in the liturgical movement. In the summer of 1938, Selle accompanied Felix Fellner to Metten and Munich, where Fellner did research on Boniface Wimmer.[145] During summer breaks, Selle spent much of his time either at Metten or Monte Cassino. "Metten," he once told me, "was one of my favorite places." At Metten, Selle was ordained deacon; he was ordained priest at Monte Cassino. In March, 1939, Selle was present in Saint Peter's Square when the joyous cry went up, *"Habemus papam!"* ("We have a pope!"). Pius XI, in his eighties and unable to walk, had died, and the cardinals met in conclave to elect his successor. To no one's surprise, they chose Pius XI's secretary of state, Eugenio Cardinal Pacelli, who took the name Pius XII. War loomed, and that threat accelerated Selle's comprehensive examinations and his departure from Sant' Anselmo.

Back at Saint Vincent, in 1940, Paulinus began his teaching career, taking the oath against Modernism. For most of his career he taught patristics and moral theology; later he taught dogmatic theology. Early in his career, Selle saw a need in his lectures on Thomas Aquinas to make clear the connection between the Redemption and the Sacraments. Selle had drawn upon Neunheuser's sense of mystery in the liturgy, a point Neunheuser (and his confrere, Odo Casel) had found in Aquinas. In all, Selle taught for fifty-seven years. From the time of the Council until his retirement in 1997, he taught liturgy. From 1955 to 1965, he served also as academic dean of the Seminary.

The span of his career is divided roughly in half by the Council. He began his career teaching in Latin, and he ended it teaching in English. "Teaching in Latin was a mistake," Father Paulinus said, explaining that "We were using theology to teach Latin, because many of the students did not have enough Latin to understand."[146] He discovered a solution to this problem. "So what I did, in order to fulfill the [canon] law, and you had to fulfill the law," he said, "was I lectured one day in Latin and the next day repeated it in English so they'd get some theology, too."[147] One student recalled, "He could take what the early church fathers said and show how it was consistent with what Vatican II was saying."[148] This approach then proved helpful when the students became priests in parishes. As priests they were able to explain the Council to the lay faithful.

Rev. Paulinus Selle, O.S.B., teaching.

According to his former students, Father Paulinus's teaching style derived from the way he had been taught in Rome, slowly reading his lecture so that the students could write down what he read. His examinations were legendary, often composed of two hundred true or false questions, each worth half a point. He was noted also for ending class promptly, when the bell rang simply closing his manila folder of lecture notes, often in mid-sentence, and leaving the classroom. The next day he would enter the classroom, open the folder, and begin precisely where he had left off the day before.

As a monk, he served as novice master and as a member of the abbot's council of seniors. As years accumulated, honors came his way. In 1989, anticipating his fiftieth anniversary of teaching, nearly two hundred alumni, colleagues, confreres, family, and friends gathered at Saint Vincent for a Mass and a dinner. "I wish I deserved this honor," Selle said, with characteristic modesty and humor, "but I will accept it."[149] In 1992, the Seminary conferred upon him an honorary doctorate, since he had been too busy teaching to pursue one.

Professional and Academic Degrees

More so than before the Council, credentials and degrees have become more important as indications of proficiency. For most of the Seminary's history, ordination to the priesthood took the place of a degree. In 1966, the Seminary began offering a Master of Divinity (M. Div.); alumni who were graduated before 1966 found that it was helpful in dealing with the secular world to have a degree from seminary. As seminaries came to be seen as not only places of pastoral formation, but also of theological graduate studies, priests, especially those seeking doctoral degrees, saw the need for some sort of academic credential from the Seminary. So, in 1973 the Seminary made available an Alumni M. Div., for which the pre-1966 alumni were eligible.

With the Second Vatican Council and its document, *Perfectae caritatis,* on the renewal of religious life, monasteries and convents had to revisit their approach to training monks, friars, and sisters. Within religious communities of men, the question focused on the integration of lay brothers with choir monks. In terms relevant to seminaries, the question meant what sort of education to require of brothers. In the days before the Council, lay brothers provided for their monasteries what could best be called blue-collar work. In that era, a monk who had the capacity for academic work yet felt no call to priesthood was sometimes seen as an underachiever, or even as a shirker of a duty to become a rainmaker, as though a monastery were a firm of priests.

Seminaries had to face this new situation without falling into the seemingly easy solution of simply demanding all monks to study the same curriculum. "The removal of the requirement that choir monks proceed to sacred orders," Claude J. Peifer has written, "has brought about a larger proportion of non-clerical juniors, in many cases no less able or academically oriented than their clerical counterparts."[150] While underscoring that "[s]eminary training can scarcely be considered an adequate substitute for a specifically monastic formation,"[151] Peifer makes clear that seminary education can give junior monks "a deeper understanding and appreciation of their vocation, so that they may be able to live it more fully and with greater profit both to themselves and to others."[152] As Fulton Sheen said of the priest, the monk is not his own.[153]

At Saint Vincent Seminary, the discussion on how best to offer theological education to monks not seeking holy orders resulted in the option of a Master of Arts degree. The Seminary had long had a Master's program on the books, including a Master's of Religious Education, but it had fallen into disuse. According to Seminary catalogues, in 1977 the Seminary began offering M. A. degrees in Sacred Scripture or Systematic Theology; later, these options included Monastic Studies. Monks outside the ordination program thus had the opportunity to study without undertaking the seven-year course leading to the M. Div. Nevertheless, the M. Div. also was an option for them, and men studying for the M. Div. could also study for one of the M. A. degrees. The Seminary's Master of Arts degrees have the option of a thesis, but required are three comprehensive examinations, two written, one oral. The written exams cover course work and a reading list, and the viva voce exam addresses both.

Twenty years later, options increased. In 1999, negotiations with the Dominican House of Studies in Washington, D. C., began, resulting in the Seminary being affiliated with that faculty.[154] Consequently, since 2000 Saint Vincent may again award the Bachelor of Sacred Theology (S. T. B.). As with the M. A., the S. T. B. culminates in written and oral comprehensive exams. Students may pursue this ecclesiastical degree by itself or concurrent with studies for the M. Div. An advantage to earning the S. T. B. is its recognition by Roman universities, so that a student who is then selected for studies, for example, at the Gregorian or Lateran universities in Rome would be more readily accepted.

New Ministries

When Boniface Wimmer first came to America, his aim was to minister to the German Catholics in western Pennsylvania. He soon found within his mission territory Irish Catholics, and in time priests from Saint Vincent had care of Catholics of Italian, Polish, and Slovak origin. Within a generation or two of immigration, these ethnic groups assimilated themselves into the wider culture of America, learning English and otherwise adapting. By the end of the twentieth century, the largest growth in population among Catholics in America was in Hispanic families. Diocesan students from large cities such as Atlanta, Georgia, and Tulsa, Oklahoma, knew they would as priests be sent to parishes with a majority of Spanish-speaking parishioners. To prepare these seminarians for their ministry, in 1991 the Seminary began a Hispanic Ministry program. By 2000, the program offered four years of classes in the Spanish language, as well as courses in Hispanic history and culture.[155]

With the number of priests declining, young priests who once had years of experience as parochial vicars find themselves becoming pastors only a few years after ordination. In some cases, a newly ordained priest is assigned at once to be a pastor. Long defunct was the accounting program run by Father Daniel Kaib, and financial matters were often foreign to seminarians. In 2003, the Seminary inaugurated a Pastoral Stewardship Program. This program began under the auspices of John Marous.

Marous is a native of Pittsburgh's North Side, where he was born in 1925. He served as a sergeant in the United States Army during the Second World War, seeing combat in Europe, and after the war he studied under the G. I. Bill at the University of Pittsburgh. There he earned a bachelor's and a master's degree in electrical engineering. In 1949, while still a graduate student, he began working for Westinghouse, based in Pittsburgh. Since 1886, when George Westinghouse founded the company, it had been a major electronics firm, for many years best known for its kitchen appliances.

Marous and his colleagues worked to emphasize the company's larger role, befitting an institution set up by the man who helped discover and develop alternating current. In 1979 Marous became president of Westinghouse's international division, his energy and efficiency earning the friendship of Henry Kissinger and Malcolm Forbes. From 1988 to 1990 Marous served as chairman and chief executive officer of Westinghouse, where he was admired as "an intuitive leader."[156]

Dr. John C. Marous, Jr.

Since 1995 John Marous has served on the Seminary's Board

of Regents, in 1998 becoming its chairman. He has applied his keen financial sense and strong instinct for leadership to the workings of the Seminary, and he has taken a personal interest in priestly formation. He and his wife have opened their country home to seminarians, once a year hosting a picnic for the new students. Although as an executive he had been described as "blunt and impatient,"[157] with a "direct and unadorned managerial style,"[158] Marous impressed the seminarians as grandfatherly and lacking pretensions. His emphasis upon "Total Quality," a phrase he brought from his days at the helm of Westinghouse, showed a straightforward zeal for excellence and integrity. When he announced the creation of the Pastoral Steward-

The Seminary's Pastoral Stewardship Program brings in experts to help train seminarians for the practical tasks of administering a parish. Participating in the program on "Leadership: Management of the Church's Financial Assets," on October 2, 2004, were, front, from left, Dr. John C. Marous, Jr., Chairman, Seminary Board of Regents; Hon. Maureen E. Lally-Green, Board of Regents; Archabbot Douglas R. Nowicki, O.S.B., Chancellor; back, from left, Rev. Justin M. Matro, O.S.B., Vice Rector and Dean of Human Formation; Very Rev. Kurt Belsole, O.S.B., Rector; Mr. Fred O'Brien, Chief Financial Officer, Diocese of Pittsburgh; Rev. Raymond Riffle, Director of Catholic Charities for the Diocese of Greensburg; Very Rev. Lawrence DiNardo, Episcopal Vicar for Canonical Services, Department for Canon and Civil Law Services, Diocese of Pittsburgh; Very Rev. Roger Statnick, Vicar General and General Executive Director of the Diocese of Greensburg; Very Rev. Paul Bradley, General Secretary and Vicar General of the Diocese of Pittsburgh; Rita Ferko Joyce, Esq., Director of the Office for Civil Legal Services for the Diocese of Pittsburgh; and John M. Lally, a certified public accountant and founding member of Lally & Lally Co., LLC.

ship Program, Marous said that he and the Board of Regents "recognized the need for increased training in the leadership and management skills necessary to function as the CEO of a parish."[159] Wise is the man who sees the difference between management of things and leadership of people.

For more than ten years John Marous has contributed generously of his time, talent, and treasure to Saint Vincent and other institutions as well. He has been involved with the Boy Scouts of America, and with the bishop of Pittsburgh, he helped establish the Extra Mile Education Foundation, providing educational opportunities for poor children of the inner city. In 1985 he and his wife endowed at the University of Pittsburgh a professorial chair in Catholicism and Christian Ethics in Contemporary Society. In 1990 Pope John Paul II made Marous a Knight of Saint Gregory the Great, and in 2006 he was named Knight Commander of the Order of Saint Gregory the Great.

The Pastoral Stewardship Program is an intensive one-day workshop. One Saturday morning a semester, ordination students attend a workshop designed to help prepare them for the practical tasks of administering a parish. During these sessions, the students hear from a variety of professionals, including accountants, attorneys, and judges. On occasion bishops, such as Bernard Schmitt of Wheeling-Charleston, and Bishop Donald Wuerl of Pittsburgh (now Archbishop of Washington, D.C.), as well as federal legislators, such as Congresswoman Melissa Hart and United States Senator Rick Santorum, have also addressed the seminarians.

Elder Brothers in the Faith

Since the Second Vatican Council and its decree *Nostra aetate*, on the Church's relations with other religions, the Seminary has also benefited from a closer association with the local Jewish community.

That association had existed before the mid-1960s, but after that point, it developed. In 1946, for example, Rabbi Solomon Freehof, of Rodef Shalom Temple, in Pittsburgh, presented Archabbot Alfred Koch with a sixteenth-century Graduale, a manuscript codex originally from Spain. The gift was to mark Saint Vincent Archabbey's one hundredth anniversary.[160] After the Council's decree, *Nostra aetate*, Freehof's ties to Saint Vincent grew. In January, 1965, at Saint Vincent, Bishop William Connare opened a three-day symposium on Jewish and Catholic theology. Freehof spoke on Saint Paul's image of Gentile believers being branches grafted onto the olive tree of Judaism (Rom 11:17-24).[161]

From 1968 until the present, Jason Z. Edelstein has taught at Saint Vincent as an adjunct professor starting in the College. In 1995 he began teaching in the Seminary as well. At first he offered

Mr. Robert Mendler

seminarians courses on Judaism, relying on the books of Martin Buber, but since the mid-1990s, he has taught pastoral counseling, drawing upon the psychological work of Viktor Frankl. Edelstein has retired as the rabbi of Temple David, in Monroeville, just east of Pittsburgh.[162]

Seminarians have also learned first-hand about the Holocaust from occasional lectures by Robert Mendler, a survivor of ten concentration camps, including Auschwitz.[163] He is a native of Nowy-Targ, Poland, a neighboring village to Wadowice, home of John Paul II. Mendler's boyhood memories include the elder Karol Wojtyla visiting the family soda fountain. When I asked him what the pope's father was like, Mendler beamed, "Just like him," meaning the pope, adding, "A big guy with a round face!" At Auschwitz he heard of the sacrifice made by Maximilian Kolbe. After liberation by United States infantrymen, Mendler came to America to seek an uncle; seventy-two members of his family had been killed by the Nazis. Mendler settled in Latrobe, where for many years he and his uncle ran a shoe store.

Ecumenical Cooperation

The population of the city of Latrobe has been predominantly Protestant, with a large number of Presbyterians. When Boniface Wimmer established a Benedictine monastery at the parish of Saint Vincent, local Protestants were wary of it. As it grew, Saint Vincent seemed to some of them to be a forbidding, if not threatening, Catholic outpost looming atop the hill outside of town. In the second half of the twentieth century, that opinion began to fade. Distrust broke down in part because of friendly dealings between local Protestant farmers and the lay brothers operating the abbey's gristmill.

As for the academic side of Saint Vincent, in 1967 the Rev. Dr. Robert R. Vogelsang, pastor of the Latrobe Presbyterian Church, began teaching biblical archaeology in the College's Religious Studies Department. Seminarians as well as collegians took his classes. In December, 1982, Vogelsang died suddenly of a heart attack; colleagues, such as Demetrius Dumm and Jason Edelstein, who had taught with Vogelsang at Saint Vincent, honored his memory with a Festschrift of essays on the Book of Exodus.[164]

Friendships between Latrobe Presbyterians and monks of Saint Vincent extended beyond the clergy. James Rogers, a local industrialist and a member of Vogelsang's congregation, was friends with Archabbot Denis Strittmatter and respected the role Saint Vincent had in the area. Rogers had grown up with the example of his father's friendship with Archabbot Alfred Koch.[165] The day of the great fire

Mr. Fred Rogers and Archabbot Douglas R. Nowicki, O.S.B.

at Saint Vincent in 1963, James Rogers came to Saint Vincent and gave Archabbot Denis a check representing an amount of some magnitude.

James Rogers's son, Fred, developed a relationship with Saint Vincent as well. In 1963, Fred Rogers became a Presbyterian minister and was a pioneer in using television for his ministry. He created a popular children's television show, "Mister Rogers' Neighborhood," in its prime airing on some three hundred public television stations across the nation. Rogers appeared on the show as himself, a calming presence for a child's often confusing day. The show used puppets and human actors to teach basic values, such as honesty and fair play, and Rogers's own low-key approach reassured children that being quiet and taking their time were virtues worth cultivating. Viewers acquainted with Benedictine monasticism could see themes Rogers had admired in the monks he had known all his life.[166]

Archabbot Douglas Nowicki, early in his priesthood, earned a doctorate in child psychology and served as a consultant to the show. In 1979, then Father Douglas organized a symposium at Saint Vincent to honor Rogers's twenty-fifth anniversary in broadcasting. In 1995 at an ecumenical Vespers service at which seminarians participated, Fred Rogers delivered the keynote address to open Saint Vincent's sesquicentennial celebrations.[167] This close and longstanding association has resulted in the establishment of the Fred M. Rogers Center on the Saint Vincent campus. This effort has been supported by many Protestant friends, such as the Mellons.

In 1979 the Seminary granted its first master's degree to a woman,

Elizabeth ("Betty") Todd, an ordained elder in the Presbyterian Church USA. Not only Protestant laity, but also clergy, have taken courses at the Seminary. During the Church's annual week of prayer for Christian unity, a local Protestant leader has addressed the seminarians. Also, Robert Duncan, bishop of the Episcopal Diocese of Pittsburgh, has been a frequent guest and occasional speaker at the Seminary.

STRUCTURAL RENOVATIONS

In 1996, as part of Saint Vincent Archabbey's sesquicentenary, the Seminary received its first new chapel.[168] Throughout its history, the Seminary had used either the old parish church of 1835 or the new abbey church of 1905. Quite often, its use of the church of 1905 (now called the basilica) was confined to the chapel in the crypt. In the 1970s, seminarian Lawrence McNeil, of the Diocese of Harrisburg, and others got permission to turn an at-

Construction of the Elizabeth J. Roderick Center

Construction of the Seminary Chapel

His Eminence Francis Cardinal Arinze celebrates Mass in the Saint Gregory Chapel

tic room in Aquinas Hall into a student chapel.

In 1996, Archabbot Douglas Nowicki broke ground for the new chapel building, to be nestled in the corner formed by Leander Hall and Gregory Hall. Simple and spare of design, the chapel was planned to seat 120 people. In 1997, the chapel was blessed and put under the patronage of the biographer of Saint Benedict, Pope Saint Gregory the Great. Presiding over the blessing was Anthony Bosco, an alumnus of the Seminary and Bishop of Greensburg. Since becoming bishop in 1979, Bosco had served on the Seminary's Board of Regents, from 1991 to 1998 serving as its chairman. The homilist was Donald Wuerl, Bishop of Pittsburgh; also present was Nicholas Dattilo, Bishop of Harrisburg and vice chairman of the Seminary's Board of Regents. Representatives of the First Catholic Slovak Ladies Association attended the Mass and subsequent dinner; the Association's beneficence helped make the chapel possible. In addition, the First Catholic Slovak Ladies Associaton established a scholarship at the Seminary, the Sväté Písmo i Katolícka Viera Endowment Fund. As well as providing for student scholarships, the Fund aids faculty research and the theological resources of the library.

Concurrent with this construction was renovation of Gregory Hall, made possible in large part by the generosity of David Roderick, former chief executive officer of USX. Given the extent of the changes to the building, the Seminary thought it appropriate to give the building a new name. In the end, the decision was to honor the memory of Mr. Roderick's late wife, Elizabeth, "a deeply religious person who was devoted to her family and to her Catholic faith."[169] The old Hall, refurbished and expanded to include offices and rooms for students and guests, became known as the Elizabeth J. Roderick Center, more commonly called Roderick Hall.

The new and expanded buildings for the Seminary were signs of growth. By the late 1990s, enrollment was again near one hundred, a number not seen since the mid-1960s. More bishops and abbots were sending their men to Saint Vincent for priestly formation, showing a confidence in the Seminary as strong as that of eighty years before, when the Seminary was sought out as a bastion against Modernism. Soon after its dedication, Saint Gregory Chapel became used for Eucharistic adoration each morning from 5:30 to 6:30. These developments put the Seminary on *Crisis* magazine's list of top seminaries.[170]

After fifty years, the Seminary's academic building began to show its age. Aquinas Hall had been adequate in the 1950s, but by the third millennium, it was found wanting. Steam radiators defied human control, forcing occupants of the classrooms to open the windows even in the middle of winter. In the midst of the relentless steam, the pipes of the radiator clanged apace, seemingly in imitation of atonal, avant-garde music.

The Renovated Aquinas Hall, now the John and Annette Brownfield Center

*The Teaching Chapel
in the Brownfield Center*

Fluorescent lighting flickered and hummed to the point of distraction, and the tiled staircase made the second floor and the basement accessible only to the able-bodied.

In 2004 renovations began.[171] In addition to improvements in the heating system, new lights were installed. Classrooms were equipped with computer ports and the apparatus necessary for Power Point® presentations. Moreover, an elevator connected all three floors. The basement level, long used only for storage, became a kind of laboratory, a mock chapel for seminarians to practice preaching, baptizing, and celebrating Mass. Throughout the building, fresh paint and new carpet enhanced the appearance, as did tasteful artwork. Classrooms were graced with framed copies of medieval manuscript leaves, and the main hallway was hung with framed prints of Giovanni Battista Piranesi's engravings of Rome in the eighteenth century.

In September, 2005, the renovated building was rededicated and renamed, commemorating the primary benefactors, the late John and Annette Brownfield. In the years before his death in

John and Annette Brownfield

1997, John Brownfield, a retired executive of Teledyne, a local steel manufacturer, had contributed to scholarships both in the College and in the Seminary, something his widow continued. Both he and his wife had lived simple, frugal lives in Latrobe, and they had attended Mass frequently at Saint Vincent, after his death her presence being almost daily. Annette Brownfield had endeared herself to the monks with her homemade fudge, both chocolate and peanut butter. Preceding the rededication was a memorial Mass for Annette Brownfield, who had passed away eight weeks before. During his homily, Archabbot Douglas Nowicki took the occasion to name her a posthumous honorary alumna of the Seminary.

WITNESS FOR HUMAN LIFE

In January, 1973, the United States Supreme Court ruled in Roe v. Wade that emanating from within the "penumbras" of the United

Seminarians at the March for Life in Washington, D.C. in 2004

States Constitution could be found a right to procure an abortion. This judicial mandate that put one person's right to liberty over another (unborn) person's right to life awakened the moral conscience of the nation. Each January after Roe v. Wade, tens of thousands of people from across America meet in Washington, D. C., to mark the anniversary of the Court's decision. The method used was borrowed from the Civil Rights Movement of the 1960s, namely a peaceful march from one point to another. In this case, the March for Life traverses Constitution Avenue, past the White House, and up Capitol Hill to the Supreme Court; the season and the location often assure marchers face icy winds and bleak skies.

Since 1990, monks and seminarians from Saint Vincent have participated in the March for Life.[172] Those seminarians remaining behind participate in other corporal works of mercy. The day itself is called Social Concerns Day, and students not going to Washington spend the day helping with Meals on Wheels, at the Latrobe area food bank, or visiting the elderly, either at a local nursing home or in the monastic infirmary. Both in Washington and in Latrobe, the seminar-

Diocesan and Benedictine seminarians in 2005

ians have occasion for Eucharistic adoration to sustain them.

These charitable works continue throughout the year, one instance being a monthly prayer vigil in front of an abortion clinic in Pittsburgh. As seminarians become more informed about the gift, not only of human sexuality, but also of celibacy, in no small way thanks to the path-breaking book by John Paul II, *The Theology of the Body* (1997), they see that embryonic human life is as sacred as that of any adult.

Twenty-first Century

In 1986, Swiss theologian Hans Urs von Balthasar was interviewed by one of his former students, Angelo Scola. Scola asked Balthasar what he observed about current seminarians and those recently ordained to priesthood. Despite different temperaments, Balthasar said, young priests he knew all had a "desire for the whole unabbreviated and unvarnished revelation of God as it was given to us in Jesus Christ," a desire driven by an equal passion that "it may be lived and taught uncompromisingly."[173] Balthasar explained that for these fervent young priests, "theologies which have been invented in 1968 or later…are no longer of interest to them," and he added, "the same holds true for any narrow-minded conservatism."[174] He summed up this new generation of priests by saying that for them, "matters which cannot be embraced in prayer are not worthy to be thought of, and even less to be preached."[175]

By and large, Balthasar's description of young priests in Europe in the mid-1980s applies fifteen and twenty years later to seminarians and newly ordained priests from Saint Vincent. A recent rector observed, "priests of tomorrow will place a definite priority upon liturgical praying and upon personal prayer," thereby "seeking an experience of intimacy with God," and then wanting to "witness to this intimacy and share it with others."[176] He added that not all will become saints, but they will strive to answer the universal call to holiness. From his observations, future priests "will face the same challenges and discouragements as well as the great joys"[177] known to previous generations of priests. Another rector has said that seminary education should, at its best, help seminarians "see that they are not individuals, but members of a larger community, tradition, and history."[178] With this realization, he concludes, future priests will derive from the Church's liturgical prayer a desire to be more self-giving.

Pope John Paul II

These personal observations by three priests well-placed to make them converge to form a composite picture. For current seminarians and the priests they become, to live and teach and preach the

Gospel without compromise is their ideal; prayer is the force driving their works of charity. With few exceptions, seminarians today were born after the Second Vatican Council, and for many, the Council is a dim memory even for their parents. Seminarians who have come to Catholicism from Protestant communities grew up with the Council as an abstraction, something belonging to another tradition.

Pope Benedict XVI

Nevertheless, these seminarians

are alive to the teaching of the Council, as found for example in *Optatam totius*. With few exceptions, these seminarians of the past quarter century have had as their primary vocation director the late Pope John Paul II. They heard his sermons and read his encyclicals and discerned a calling to serve the Church as priests. The election on 19 April, 2005, to the Chair of Peter of Joseph Cardinal Ratzinger, long so closely associated with John Paul II, was greeted by most of the seminarians at Saint Vincent with jubilation. [179] They had long used his books in their classes and for their spiritul reading, and "he was one of their unsung heroes." [180]

On the evening of Ratzinger's election as Pope Benedict XVI, seminarians gathered in their chapel to chant the *Te Deum*. Although this celebration had been planned, there was a palpable joy among the seminarians. In no small part, this joy came from the seminarians believing they saw in that papal election an assurance of

Bishop Lawrence E. Brandt, J.C.D., Ph.D.

continuity with the work begun by John Paul II. Seminarians took the election of Benedict XVI as a sign that John Paul II's interpretation of the Second Vatican Council would remain alive.

The Seminary took swift measures to keep this dream alive. Lawrence Brandt, Bishop of Greensburg and longtime member of the Seminary's Board of Regents, explained that the Board had seen the

129

need to integrate liturgy and Scripture in order to improve the quality of preaching. In November, 2005, the Seminary inaugurated the Benedict XVI Chair of Biblical Theology and Liturgical Proclamation. It is the first professorial chair in the world named in honor of Pope Benedict XVI, and in September, 2005, Archabbot Douglas had an audience with the Pope asking his blessing for such an academic honor. The first holder of this chair is Dr. Scott Hahn, for fifteen years a professor at the Franciscan University of Steubenville, Ohio. His inaugural lecture, given before several hundred people, was published in *Origins*. [181]

In 2000, he had been a visiting professor at Saint Vincent Seminary. Hahn, a native of Pittsburgh, was a Presbyterian minister, and he had taught at Chesapeake Theological Seminary, now merged into the Reformed Theological Seminary of Washington, D. C. In 1986 Hahn's studies of Scripture and the Fathers of the Church made him feel inexorably drawn to the Catholic Church. He and his wife describe their conversions to Catholicism in their best-selling memoir, *Rome Sweet Home*.[182]

Since then, Hahn has become one of the most visible Catholic converts in America. Among American literary converts of the twentieth century, he takes his place with Thomas Merton and Avery Dulles. Hahn, an impassioned speaker with a gift for extemporizing, has

Dr. Scott Hahn

Dr. Scott Hahn giving the inaugural lecture of the Pope Benedict XVI
Chair of Biblical Theology and Liturgical Proclamation on November 28, 2005

appeared frequently on television, notably on the EWTN channel, and he has spoken to various conferences and retreats, five hundred of his talks having become available on audiotape or compact disc. As an apologist, he has written essays for Catholic magazines such as *This Rock* and *Envoy*, but as a scholar, he has written articles for *The Catholic Biblical Quarterly*, his research focusing on Christianity's roots in Judaism and their common bond of covenant and sacrifice. In 1999 he wrote the foreword to the English translation of Joseph Ratzinger's *Many Religions, One Covenant: Israel, the Church, and the World.*

Hahn has written half a dozen popular books of theology, addressing the sacraments and the Blessed Virgin Mary. With Mike Aquilina he compiled *Living the Mysteries*, an anthology of writings from seven of the Church Fathers. In late 2005 Hahn published *Letter and Spirit*, dedicated to his seminarians, a more specialized yet still highly readable study of the relationship between Scripture and liturgy. These themes have long captured the attention of Pope Benedict, himself author of a profound but lucid work, *The Spirit of the Liturgy* (2000).

Hahn is thus uniquely prepared to teach and discuss the Christian heritage. He draws not only upon his pastoral experience, but also his sectarian training as a Protestant and his doctoral education at Marquette University in Catholic theology. After years of study and discernment, he can see from within the two great traditions of Western Christianity. In addition to the Augustinian extrapolations of John Calvin and Karl Barth, Hahn has a command of the Bible and the Church Fathers, as well as the great flowering of orthodox Catholic theology from Thomas Aquinas to Pope Benedict XVI.

As George Weigel, biographer of John Paul II, told the Seminary's graduates in 2000, the Council saw that "updating must always proceed from…a return to the sources of Christian wisdom in Scripture, the Fathers, and the medieval masters."[183] The liturgical, patristic, and scriptural renewals that informed the Fathers of the Council also inform—from within—today's seminarians. From their study of theology, they find within themselves the indelible baptismal mark of the Holy Trinity. They learn and accept that Christianity is a religion of giving and receiving, and they are eager to give of themselves in order to hand on the revealed truths they have received.

Appendices

Rectors

Note: The abbot of Saint Vincent is also chancellor of the Seminary, and until 1914 the Seminary, while enjoying that name, functioned *de facto* as a department of the College, the "director" being a monk priest who taught in the College. In 1914, Pope Pius X granted the Seminary pontifical status, and with it the director became officially the rector. In 1852, Boniface Wimmer named Demetrius di Marogna, O. S. B., rector; hence the gap between Di Marogna and Vitus Kratzer, O. S. B.

Demetrius di Marogna, O. S. B. (1852-1856)
Vitus Kratzer, O. S. B. (1914-1916)
Ambrose Kohlbeck, O. S. B. (1916-1931)
John Nepomucene Hruza, O. S. B. (1931-1952)
Oliver A. Grosselin, O. S. B. (1952-1963)
Demetrius R. Dumm, O. S. B. (1963-1980)
John E. Haag, O. S. B. (1980-1989)
Thomas Acklin, O. S. B. (1989-2000)
Kurt Belsole, O. S. B. (2000-2006)
Justin Matro, O.S.B. (2006-present)

Enrollment

Note: The following statistics give the number of ordination students for a given academic year. For the years 1865 to 1938, figures come from Anselm Ober's thesis, "An Historical Sketch of the Establishment and Development of St. Vincent Seminary;" for 1938 to 1964, from Seminary catalogues for those years. From 1964 to the present, with lacunae as indicated (NA, not available), records exist in the office of the Seminary's academic dean.

In 1846, Boniface Wimmer taught four men studying for priesthood; the Seminary's formal records began in 1865. One notices a steady increase, with larger numbers during the First World War, when bishops could not send men for studies in Rome. After the First World War, mainly in response to the crisis over Modernism, enrollment remained over one hundred. In 1942 it dropped to eighty-eight, rising the next year over one hundred, then dropping below one hundred until the early 1950s. A sharp decrease came in the wake of the Second Vatican Council; numbers rose again during the pontificate of John Paul II.

1865-1866	11	1876-1877	46	1887-1888	57
1866-1867	6	1877-1878	37	1888-1889	50
1867-1868	13	1878-1879	35	1889-1890	48
1868-1869	14	1879-1880	36	1890-1891	57
1869-1870	13	1880-1881	42	1891-1892	45
1870-1871	11	1881-1882	42	1892-1893	51
1871-1872	15	1882-1883	42	1893-1894	47
1872-1873	25	1883-1884	39	1894-1895	49
1873-1874	26	1884-1885	34	1895-1896	46
1874-1875	33	1885-1886	38	1896-1897	46
1875-1876	30	1886-1887	44	1897-1898	43

1898-1899	45	1934-1935	161	1970-1971	74
1899-1900	50	1935-1936	159	1971-1972	70
1900-1901	45	1936-1937	127	1972-1973	54
1901-1902	41	1937-1938	115	1973-1974	53
1902-1903	39	1938-1939	124	1974-1975	48
1903-1904	41	1939-1940	138	1975-1976	50
1904-1905	44	1940-1941	121	1976-1977	55
1905-1906	55	1941-1942	112	1977-1983	NA
1906-1907	53	1942-1943	88	1983-1984	46
1907-1908	65	1943-1944	109	1984-1985	52
1908-1909	53	1944-1945	90	1985-1986	53
1909-1910	54	1945-1946	80	1986-1987	53
1910-1911	58	1946-1947	53	1987-1988	54
1911-1912	50	1947-1948	52	1988-1989	50
1912-1913	53	1948-1949	57	1989-1990	38
1913-1914	63	1949-1950	58	1990-1991	51
1914-1915	84	1950-1951	57	1991-1992	58
1915-1916	77	1951-1952	67	1992-1993	67
1916-1917	89	1952-1953	90	1993-1994	63
1917-1918	107	1953-1954	115	1994-1995	61
1918-1919	110	1954-1955	126	1995-1996	69
1919-1920	127	1955-1956	136	1996-1997	75
1920-1921	138	1956-1957	129	1997-1998	84
1921-1922	140	1957-1958	120	1998-1999	95
1922-1923	124	1958-1959	122	1999-2000	97
1923-1924	129	1959-1960	110	2000-2001	96
1924-1925	113	1960-1961	NA	2001-2002	87
1925-1926	142	1961-1962	NA	2002-2003	76
1926-1927	147	1962-1963	120	2003-2004	70
1927-1928	153	1963-1964	NA	2004-2005	61
1928-1929	159	1964-1965	117	2005-2006	68
1929-1930	165	1965-1966	122		
1930-1931	148	1966-1967	119		
1931-1932	135	1967-1968	69		
1932-1933	158	1968-1969	78		
1933-1934	148	1969-1970	82		

Distinguished Alumni

Note: This list of prelates gives years of service. It does not include members of the hierarchy who have had honorary degrees conferred by the Seminary. In all, there have been twenty-one bishops or archbishops, one of whom was also a cardinal; of the twenty-eight abbots or archabbots, one also served as an archbishop.

Diocesan Clergy

Anthony Bosco, Bishop of Greensburg, Pennsylvania (1987-2004)

Hugh C. Boyle, Bishop of Pittsburgh, Pennsylvania (1921-1950)

J. F. Regis Canevin, Bishop of Pittsburgh, Pennsylvania (1903-1921)

William Connare, Bishop of Greensburg, Pennsylvania (1960-1987)

Joseph B. Cotter, Bishop of Winona, Minnesota (1889-1909)

Nicholas C. Dattilo, Bishop of Harrisburg, Pennsylvania (1989-2004) *

Norbert Gaughan, Auxiliary Bishop of Greensburg, Pennsylvania (1975-1984); Bishop of Gary, Indiana (1984-1996)

Rene H. Gracida, Auxiliary Bishop of Miami, Florida (1971-1975); Bishop of Pensacola-Tallahassee, Florida (1975-1983); Bishop of Corpus Christi, Texas (1983-1997)

Edward G. Hettinger, Auxiliary Bishop of Columbus, Ohio (1941-1977)

John B. McDowell, Auxiliary Bishop of Pittsburgh, Pennsylvania (1966-present)

James A. McFaul, Bishop of Trenton, New Jersey (1894-1917)

George Mundelein, Cardinal Archbishop of Chicago, Illinois (1915-1939)

Joseph Rademacher, Bishop of Fort Wayne, Indiana (1883-1900)

Michael J. Ready, Bishop of Columbus, Ohio (1944-1957)

Joseph Schrembs, Bishop of Cleveland, Ohio (1911-1945)

James Trobec, Bishop of Saint Cloud, Minnesota (1897-1921)

John Ambrose Watterson, Bishop of Columbus, Ohio (1880-1899)
William J. Winter, Auxiliary Bishop of Pittsburgh, Pennsylvania (1988-2005)

* Nicholas C. Dattilo was an alumnus of Saint Vincent College and Saint Charles Borromeo Seminary, Overbrook, Pennsylvania; as was the case with Saint Vincent, Saint Charles did not then grant degrees. Consequently, Dattilo requested and received an Alumni M. Div. from Saint Vincent.

Religious Clergy

Cyprian Bradley, O. S. B., Abbot of Holy Cross Abbey, Canon City, Colorado (1926-1931)
Bertrand Dolan, O. S. B., Abbot of Saint Anselm Abbey, Manchester, New Hampshire (1927-1968)
Egbert Donovan, O. S. B., Archabbot of Saint Vincent Archabbey, Latrobe, Pennsylvania (1967-1979)
Alexius Edelbrock, O. S. B., Abbot of Saint John's Abbey, Collegeville, Minnesota (1875-1908)
Peter Engel, O. S. B., Abbot of Saint John's Abbey, Collegeville, Minnesota (1895-1921)
Louis M. Fink, O. S. B., Bishop of Leavenworth, Kansas (1871-1904)
Leo Haid, O. S. B., Vicar Apostolic of North Carolina and Abbot Nullius of Belmont Abbey, North Carolina (1888-1924)
Ernest Helmstetter, O. S. B., Abbot of Saint Mary's Abbey, Newark, New Jersey (1910-1929)
Corbinian Hofmeister, O. S. B., Abbot of Saint Michael's Abbey, Metten, Germany (1929-1966); survived imprisonment in Dachau under the Nazis, April 1944-April 1945
Vincent Huber, O. S. B., Abbot of Saint Bede's, Peru, Illinois (1910-1941)
Nepomucene Jaeger, O. S. B., Abbot of Saint Procopius Abbey, Lisle, Illinois (1894-1924)
Valentine Kohlbeck, O. S. B., Abbot of Saint Procopius Abbey, Lisle, Illinois (1919-1937)
Boniface Krug, O. S. B., Archabbot of Monte Cassino, Italy; (1897-1909)
Leopold Krul, O. S. B., Archabbot of Saint Vincent Archabbey, Latrobe,

Pennsylvania (1979-1983)

Paul R. Maher, O. S. B., Archabbot of Saint Vincent Archabbey, Latrobe, Pennsylvania (1983-1990)

Cuthbert McDonald, O. S. B., Abbot of Saint Benedict's Abbey, Atchison, Kansas (1943-1962)

Bernard Menges, O. S. B., Abbot of Saint Bernard's Abbey, Cullman, Alabama (1904-1933)

Charles Mohr, O. S. B., Abbot of Saint Leo Abbey, Florida (1902-1931)

Procopius Neuzil, O. S. B., Abbot of Saint Procopius Abbey, Lisle, Illinois (1937-1946)

Douglas R. Nowicki, O. S. B., Archabbot of Saint Vincent Archabbey, Latrobe, Pennsylvania (1990-present)

Patrick O'Brien, O. S. B., Abbot of Saint Mary's Abbey, Newark, New Jersey (1937-1967)

Hilary Pfrängle, O. S. B., Abbot of Saint Mary's Abbey, Newark, New Jersey (1886-1909)

Leonard Schwinn, O. S. B., Abbot of Holy Cross Abbey, Canon City, Colorado (1937-1976)

Rupert Seidenbusch, O. S. B., Bishop of Saint Cloud, Minnesota (1875-1895)

Boniface Seng, O. S. B., Abbot of Saint Bernard's Abbey, Cullman, Alabama (1939-1957)

Denis Strittmatter, O. S. B., Archabbot of Saint Vincent Archabbey, Latrobe, Pennsylvania (1949-1963)

Lawrence Vohs, O. S. B., Abbot of Saint Bede Abbey, Peru, Illinois (1942-1969)

Rembert G. Weakland, O. S. B., Archabbot of Saint Vincent Archabbey (1963-1967); Abbot primate (1967-1977); Archbishop of Milwaukee, Wisconsin (1977-2003)

Justus Wirth, O.S.B., Abbot of Saint Bede's Abbey, Peru, Illinois (1926-1942)

Innocent Wolf, O. S. B., Abbot of Saint Benedict's Abbey, Atchison, Kansas (1877-1922)

James Zilliox, O. S. B., Abbot of Saint Mary's Abbey, Newark, New Jersey (1885-1890)

BIBLIOGRAPHY

UNPUBLISHED SOURCES

Boosel, Brian D. "Boniface Wimmer, O. S. B., and the Foundation of Saint Vincent Seminary," M. A. Thesis, Slippery Rock University, 2004.

[Ganns, H. G.], "Fugitive Recollections, Musical and Unmusical, 1868-1878, by an Old Alumnus." Typescript, Archives of Saint Vincent Archabbey.

Ober, Anselm Anthony, "An Historical Sketch of the Establishment and Development of St. Vincent Seminary." B. A. Thesis, Saint Vincent College, 1938.

Selle, Paulinus Jerome. "Building Constructions at St. Vincent," B. A. Thesis, Saint Vincent College, 1936.

Taylor, Paul Roger. "Boniface Wimmer and Saint Vincent College: The Beginning of American Benedictine Education," Ph. D. Dissertation, Boston College, 1998.

PUBLISHED SOURCES

BOOKS

Abbott, Walter M., ed. *The Documents of Vatican II.* New York: Herder and Herder, 1966.

Acklin, Thomas. *The Unchanging Heart of the Priesthood: A Faith Perspective on the Mystery and Reality of Priesthood in the Church.* Steubenville, OH: Emmaus Road Publishing, 2005.

Acta et Decreta Concilii Plenarii Baltimorensis Tertii. Baltimore: John Murphy,

1886.

Almagno, R. Stephen, ed. *Resonare Christum: A Selection from the Sermons, Addresses, Interviews, and Papers of Cardinal John Wright*, vol. 3. San Francisco: Ignatius Press, 1995.

Bekes, Gerardo J., ed. *Sant' Anselmo: Saggi Storici e di Attualità*. Rome: Sant' Anselmo, 1988.

Benson, Maxine, ed. *From Pittsburgh to the Rocky Mountains: Major Stephen Long's Expedition, 1819-1820*. Golden, CO: Fulcrum, Inc., 1988.

Butko, Brian A. *Pennsylvania Traveler's Guide: The Lincoln Highway*. Mechanicsburg, PA: Stackpole Books, 1996.

Canevin, Regis. *The Church Year: Its Seasons, Feasts, Fasts, Devotions, and Other Observances*. Union City, N. J. : The Sign Press, 1928.

Catholic Pittsburgh's One Hundred Years. Chicago: Loyola University Press, 1943.

Cox, James R. *Illustrated Lectures: 15 Minute Sermons Cut to One Minute*. Pittsburgh: The Catholic Observer, n. d.

Dawson, Christopher. *The Crisis of Western Education*. New York: Sheed and Ward, 1961.

Delatte, Paul. *The Rule of Saint Benedict: A Commentary*, trans. by Justin McCann. Latrobe, PA: The Archabbey Press, 1959.

Dolan, Jay P. *The American Catholic Experience: A History from Colonial Times to the Present*. Garden City, NY: Doubleday, 1985.

Dumm, Demetrius. *Cherish Christ Above All: The Bible in the Rule of Benedict*. New York: Paulist Press, 1996.

Ellis, John Tracy. *American Catholicism*. 2nd ed. Chicago: University of Chicago Press, 1969.

_____. *Essays in Seminary Education*. Notre Dame: Fides Publishers, 1967.

Engelbert, Pius. *Geschichte des Bendiktinerkollegs St. Anselm in Rom*. Rome: Sant' Anselmo, 1988.

50 Years on the Journey: Diocese of Greensburg, 1951-2001. Supplement to *The Catholic Accent* (8 March, 2001).

First Synod of the Diocese of Greensburg. Greensburg: Diocese of Greensburg, 1963.

Flannery, Austin, ed. *Vatican Council II*, vol. 1. Northport, NY: Costello Publishing Co., 1996.

Glenn, Francis A. *Shepherds of the Faith: 1843-1993: A Brief History of the*

Bishops of the Catholic Diocese of Pittsburgh. Pittsburgh: Catholic Diocese of Pittsburgh, 1993.

Hahn, Scott, and Hahn, Kimberly. *Rome Sweet Home: Our Journey to Catholicism.* San Francisco: Ignatius Press, 1993.

Hanley, Thomas O'Brien, ed. *The John Carroll Papers*, vol. 2. Notre Dame: University of Notre Dame Press, 1976.

Heineman, Kenneth J. *A Catholic New Deal: Religion and Reform in Depression Pittsburgh.* University Park: Pennsylvania State University Press, 1999.

Hennesey, James. *American Catholics: A History of the Roman Catholic Community in the United States.* New York: Oxford University Press, 1981.

_____. *The First Council of the Vatican: The American Experience.* New York: Herder and Herder, 1963.

Hollingsworth, Amy. *The Simple Faith of Mister Rogers: Spiritual Insights from the World's Most Beloved Neighbor.* Nashville: Integrity Publishers, 2005.

Iannetta, Sabatino. *Henry W. Longfellow and Montecassino.* Boston: B. Humphries, 1940.

Jenkins, Philip. *Hoods and Shirts: The Extreme Right in Pennsylvania, 1925-1950.* Chapel Hill: The University of North Carolina Press, 1997.

_____. *The New Anti-Catholicism: The Last Acceptable Prejudice.* New York: Oxford University Press, 2003.

Kantowicz, Edward R. *Corporation Sole: Cardinal Mundelein and Chicago Catholicism.* Notre Dame: University of Notre Dame Press, 1983.

Kline, Omer U. *The Sportsman's Hall Parish Later Named Saint Vincent, 1790-1846.* Latrobe, PA: Saint Vincent Archabbey Press, 1990.

Kollar, Rene. *Saint Vincent Archabbey and Its Role in the Development of Slovak-American Culture and History.* Latrobe, PA: Archabbey Publications, 1996.

_____. *A Universal Appeal: Aspects of the Revival of Monasticism in the West in the 19th and Early 20th Centuries.* San Francisco: International Scholars Publications, 1996.

Lee, James Michael, and Putz, Louis J., eds. *Seminary Education in a Time of Change.* Notre Dame: Fides Publishers, 1965.

Longfellow: Poetical Works. New York: Oxford University Press, 1979.

Macko, Hubert A. *Grammar of the Slovak Language*. Scranton: Obrana, 1926.

McCollester, Charles J., ed. *Fighter With a Heart: Writings of Charles Owen Rice, Pittsburgh Labor Priest*. Pittsburgh: University of Pittsburgh Press, 1996.

McCullough, David G. *The Johnstown Flood*. New York: Simon and Schuster, 1968.

McGeever, Patrick J. *Rev. Charles Owen Rice: Apostle of Contradiction*. Pittsburgh: Duquesne University Press, 1989.

Mommsen, Theodor. *The Provinces of the Roman Empire from Caesar to Diocletian*, trans. by William P. Dickson, vol. 1. London: Macmillan, 1909.

Mundelein, George William. *Two Crowded Years*. Chicago: Extension Press, 1918.

Nell-Breuning, Oswald von. *Reorganization of Social Economy*, trans. by Bernard W. Dempsey. Milwaukee: The Bruce Publishing Co., 1936.

Newman, John Henry. *Historical Sketches*. 3 London: Longmans, Green, and Co, 1913.

Novak, Michael. *The Open Church: Vatican II, Act II*. New York: Macmillan Co., 1964.

Oetgen, Jerome. *An American Abbot: Boniface Wimmer, 1809-1887*. 2nd ed. Washington, D. C.: The Catholic University of America Press, 1997.

_____. *Mission to America: A History of Saint Vincent Archabbey, the First Benedictine Monastery in the United States*. Washington, D. C.: The Catholic University of America Press, 2000.

Pegis, Anton C. *The Middle Ages and Philosophy: Some Reflections on the Ambivalence of Modern Scholasticism*. Chicago: Henry Regnery Co., 1963.

Pennacchi, Joseph. *De Honorii I Romani Pontificis Causa in Concilio VI*. Regensburg: F. Pustet, 1870.

Ratzinger, Joseph. *God and the World: Believing and Living in Our Time, a Conversation with Peter Seewald*, trans. by Henry Taylor. San Francisco: Ignatius Press, 2002.

Rippinger, Joel. *The Benedictine Order in the United States: An Interpretive History*. Collegeville: The Liturgical Press, 1990.

Röpke, Wilhelm. *A Humane Economy: The Social Framework of the Free*

Market, trans. by Elizabeth Henderson. Chicago: Henry
Regnery Co., 1960.

Scharper, Philip, ed. *Torah and Gospel: Jewish and Catholic Theology in Dialogue*. New York: Sheed and Ward, 1966.

Scola, Angelo. *Test Everything, Hold Fast to What Is Good: An Interview with Hans Urs von Balthasar*. San Francisco: Ignatius Press, 1989.

Sheen, Fulton J. *The Priest Is Not His Own*. New York: McGraw-Hill Book Co., 1963.

Southern, R. W. *Western Society and the Church in the Middle Ages*. New York: Penguin Books, 1970.

Stubbs, William, ed. *Keeping the Day: Contemplations of the Book of Exodus: A Festschrift Honoring Reverend Robert Vogelsang, D. D., 1926-1982*. Allison Park, PA: Pickwick Publications, 1985.

Syme, Ronald. *Tacitus*, vol. 1 Oxford: Clarendon Press, 1958.

Tanner, Norman P., ed. *Decrees of the Ecumenical Councils*, vol. 2 Washington, D. C.: Georgetown University Press, 1990.

Vogüé, Adalbert de, ed. *Gregory the Great: The Life of Saint Benedict*, trans. by Hilary Costello and Eoin de Bhaldraith. Petersham, MA: St. Bede's Publications, 1993.

Wissolik, Richard David, et al., eds. *Listen to Our Words: Oral Histories of the Jewish Community of Westmoreland County, Pennsylvania*. Latrobe, PA: Saint Vincent College, 1997.

Yzermans, Vincent A., ed. *American Participation in the Second Vatican Council*. New York: Sheed and Ward, 1967.

Zeller, Hubert van. *The Benedictine Idea*. London: Burns & Oates, 1959.

ARTICLES

Acklin, Thomas. "Tomorrow's Priests," *The Priest* 54 (December, 1998): 41-43.

"Address by the Rt. Rev. Bishop," *St. Vincent College Journal* 30 (December, 1920): 89-90.

Albareda, Anselm M. "Origins of Benedictine Schools, Scriptoria, and Libraries," *The Catholic Library World* 29 (May-June, 1958): 447-450.

"Archabbey's Scripture Scholar Called Suddenly by Death," *The St. Vincent Journal* 59 (September, 1949): 2.

Bagehot, Walter. "The Political Aspect of the Oecumenical Council," in Norman
     St. John Stevas, ed., *The Collected Works of Walter Bagehot* 8 (London:
     The Economist, 1974): 169-172.

Barry, Colman J. "Boniface Wimmer, Pioneer of the American Benedictines,"
     The Catholic Historical Review 41 (October, 1955): 272-296.

Belsole, Kurt. "Fatherhood from the Heart of the Church," *National Catholic
     Register* (18-24 June, 2006): 9.

_____. "A Sense of Gratitude and Accomplishment," *Leaven* 12
     (Spring, 2004): 4.

_____. "Stewards of the Mysteries: Training Seminarians for
     Liturgical Leadership," *Antiphon* 8 (2003): 22-27.

Benson, Betsy. "Men in Black," *Pittsburgh* (April, 2004): 64-83.
     "Bishop William Connare of Greensburg, a Pittsburgh Priest," *The
     Pittsburgh Catholic* (16 June, 1995): 12.

Bridge, Gerard. "The Rt. Rev. George Mundelein, D. D.: Archbishop-Elect of
     Chicago," *St. Vincent College Journal* 25 (January, 1915): 236-239.

"Cardinal Albareda," *The Tablet* (30 July, 1966): 879-880.

"Catholics & Chance," *Time* (27 December, 1937): 24.

"Commencement Address on John Paul II's Papacy," *Leaven* 9
     (Summer/Fall, 2000): 1, 14-15, 17.

Coode, Thomas H., and John D. Petrarulo. "The Odyssey of Pittsburgh's Father
     Cox," *The Western Pennsylvania Historical Magazine* 55 (July, 1972): 217-
     238.

Cummins, Patrick. "Rev. Justin Krellner, O. S. B.: In Memoriam" *The Catholic
     Biblical Quarterly* 12 (January, 1950): 90.

Dawson, Christopher. "American Education and Christian Culture,"
     The American Benedictine Review 9 (Spring-Summer, 1958): 7-16.

DeGregorio, Scott. "Bede's *In Ezram et Neemiam* and the Reform of the
     Northumbrian Church." *Speculum* 79 (January, 2004): 1-25.

DiIanni, Albert. "A View of Religious Vocations," *America* (28 February, 1998):
8-12.

Dulles, Avery. "*Centesimus Annus* and the Renewal of Culture," *Journal of
     Markets & Morality* 2 (Spring, 1999): 1-7.

Edelstein, Jason Z. "The Saint Vincent Touch," in Campion P. Gavaler, ed.,

Saint Vincent: A Benedictine Place. (Latrobe, PA: Saint Vincent Archabbey, 1995): 35.

Edie, Callistus. "Demetrius di Marogna," *The Scriptorium* 9 (Easter, 1949): 7-30.

"Elizabeth J. Roderick Center, Chapel of Saint Gregory the Great Dedicated," *Leaven* 7 (Fall, 1997): 1, 5, 9.

"The Episcopal Change," *The Seminarists' Symposium* 3 (1920-1921): 116-117.

Erkel, R. Todd. "How John Marous Sets the Pace," *Pitt Magazine* (December, 1989): 20-24.

"Extensive Renovation and Addition of Seminary Building Completed Through the Generosity of Mrs. Annette Brownfield," *Leaven* 13 (Fall, 2004): 4-7.

Fellner, Felix. "Archabbot Boniface Wimmer as an Educator," *The National Benedictine Educational Association Bulletin* 25 (December, 1942): 3-32.

_____. "Boniface Wimmer," *The Dictionary of American Biography* 20 New York: Charles Scribner's Sons, 1936, 370-371.

_____. "The 'Two Cities' of Otto of Freising and Its Influence on the Catholic Philosophy of History," *The Catholic Historical Review* 20 (July, 1934): 154-174.

"Father Patrick Cummins, O. S. B.," *The Catholic Biblical Quarterly* 30 (April, 1968): 240-241.

"Father Paulinus Celebrates 50 Years of Teaching," *Leaven* 1 (Spring, 1989): 1.

"Father Paulinus Retires after 57 Consecutive Years Teaching," *Leaven* 7 (Fall, 1997): 1, 16.

"Fr. Anselm A. Ober, O. S. B.," *Saint Vincent* 34 (Fall, 2000): 27.

Franko, John. "Champion of Justice," *The Pittsburgh Catholic* (25 November, 2005): 12.

Hahn, Scott, "Scripture and the Liturgy: Inseparably United," *Origins* 35 (16 March, 2006): 648-653.

Heisey, Daniel J. "Cardinal Newman and Benedictine Education," *Newman Studies Journal* 1 (Fall, 2004): 38-47.

_____. "The Estate of Peter Helbron," *Cumberland County History* 21 (Summer, 2004): 23-33.

_____. "The Works of Henry Ganss," *Cumberland County History* 21 (Summer, 2004): 13-22.

"Hispanic Ministries Program Expanding," *Leaven* 9 (Summer/Fall, 2000): 4-5.

Hodge, Charles. "Letter to Pope Pius IX," *The Banner of Truth* (April, 1998):

22-25.

Hume, George Basil, "Archabbey of St Vincent's, Latrobe, USA, 11 June, 1980," *In Praise of Benedict* (London: Hodder and Stoughton, 1981): 43-48.

"Into the Mystic with John," *U. S. Catholic* 68 (April, 2003): 16-20.

Jenkins, Philip. "The Ku Klux Klan in Pennsylvania, 1920-1940," *The Western Pennsylvania Historical Magazine* 69 (April, 1986): 121-137.

Kollar, Rene. "Plans for an 18th-Century Benedictine Settlement in Western Pennsylvania: Bishop John Carroll and the English Benedictine Congregation," *Word and Spirit* 14 (1992): 3-11.

Loughlin, James F. "The Higher and Lower Education of the American Priesthood," *The American Catholic Quarterly Review* 15 (January, 1890): 101-122.

Marous, Jr., John C. "Focus on Pastoral Stewardship," *Leaven* 11 (Spring, 2002): n. p.

McGinn, Daniel. "Everybody's Next-door Neighbor," *Newsweek* (10 March, 2003): 61.

Meaney, Peter J. "Valiant Chaplain of the Bloody Tenth," *Tennessee Historical Quarterly* 41 (Spring, 1982): 37-47.

Metzgar, Kim. "Inaugural Lecture of the Pope Benedict XVI Chair of Biblical Theology and Liturgical Proclamation Given by Dr. Scott Hahn," *Leaven* 14 *Spring, 2006): 2-4.

Miles, Gregory L. "How Westinghouse Is Revving Up After the Rebound," *Business Week* (28 March, 1988): 46-52.

"Msgr. Charles Owen Rice Honored," *Leaven* 13 (Fall, 2004): 32.

"Notes and Comments," *The Catholic Historical Review* 49 (April, 1963): 147.

Olsen, Glenn W. "American Culture and Liberal Ideology in the Thought of Christopher Dawson," *Communio* 22 (Fall, 1995): 702-720.

_____. "The Benedictine Way of Life: Yesterday, Today, and Tomorrow," *Communio* 11 (Spring, 1984): 35-45.

Paris, Barry. "Reflections on a Lifetime Steeped in Books," *The Pittsburgh Post-Gazette* (13 December, 1982): 25, 30.

Pegis, Anton. "Gerald Bernard Phelan," 27 *Mediaeval Studies* (1965): i-v.

Peifer, Claude J. "The Formation of Non-Clerical Junior Monks," *The American Benedictine Review* 33 (March, 1982): 30-46.

Phelan, Gerald B. "The Pontifical Institute of Mediaeval Studies at Toronto," *The Dublin Review* 481 (Autumn, 1959): 221-234.

Pickar, Charles H. "Biblical News," *The Catholic Biblical Quarterly* 1 (July, 1939): 267-271.

Plaisance, Aloysius. "Emmeran Bliemel, O. S. B., Heroic Confederate Chaplain," *The American Benedictine Review* 17 (June, 1966): 209-216.

"Pontifical Degree Status Attained," *Leaven* 9 (Winter, 2000): 1, 4.

"Priests Members in Bible Society," *Saint Vincent Journal* 48 (15 February, 1939): 3.

"Professor Emeritus Celebrates 90th," *Leaven* 12 (Spring, 2004): 16.

"Pro-Life Activities Intensify," *Leaven* 2 (Spring, 1990): 1.

Purcell, Christine Stark. "My Son the Monk," *St. Anthony Messenger* 110 (June, 2002): 12-16.

"Rabbi Presents Ancient Missal at Academic Dinner," *The Saint Vincent Journal* 56 (September, 1946): 26.

Reilly, Matthew V. "Finding Their Way Home," *Homiletic & Pastoral Review* 94 (June, 1994): 74-76.

"Resignation of Bishop Canevin," *St. Vincent College Journal* 30 (January, 1921): 113-114.

Reuss, Francis X. "Leaves from the Diary of Francis X. Reuss, '67-'69," *St. Vincent College Journal* 18 (June, 1909): 435-439.

"The Rev. Vitus Kratzer, O. S. B.," *St. Vincent College Journal* 26 (December, 1916): 183-188.

"The Rev. Vitus Kratzer, O. S. B., J. C. D., D. D.," *The Seminarists' Symposium* 1 (1918-1919): 81.

Rice, Charles Owen. "Latrobe Seminary 'Tough and Tolerant'," *The Pittsburgh Catholic* (17 April, 1992): 5.

_____. "Remembering Fr. James R. Cox," *The Pittsburgh Catholic* (15 December, 1989): 5.

"Right Rev. Boniface Krug, O. S. B., Archabbot of Monte Cassino, Italy." *St. Vincent College Journal* 19 (October, 1909): 1-8.

"The Rt. Rev. George W. Mundelein, D. D., '92," *St. Vincent College Journal* 19 (October, 1909): 38-40.

Rogers, Fred M. "The Final Word Is Love," in Campion P. Gavaler, ed., *Saint Vincent: A Benedictine Place*. (Latrobe, PA: Saint Vincent Archabbey, 1995): 25-26.

Schmandt, Raymond H. "The Friendship Between Bishop Regis Canevin of Pittsburgh and Dr. Lawrence Flick of Philadelphia," *The Western*

Pennsylvania Historical Magazine 61 (October, 1978): 283-300.

Schuster, Mary Faith. "Father Patrick Cummins (1880-1968)," *The American Benedictine Review* 19 (March, 1968): 112-115.

Schwab, Theresa. "Why We Give," *Quarterly* 2 (Spring, 2004): 4-10

"Seminary Guest Speakers," *Leaven* 11 (Spring, 2002): 26.

"Sesquicentennial Opens," *The Benedictine Monks of Saint Vincent Archabbey Monastery Newsletter* 8 (Spring/Summer, 1995): 1-5.

Simmons, Eden. "America's Top Seminaries," *Crisis* (October, 1997): 34.

Stevens, Clifford. "The Saga of Conception Abbey," *Homiletic & Pastoral Review* 73 (January, 1973): 28-32, 44.

Stimpson, Emily. "Tomorrow's Priests Will Be 'Very Good Fruit,' Rector Says," *Our Sunday Visitor* (7 May, 2006): 7.

Weigel, George. "Re-Viewing Vatican II: An Interview with George A. Lindbeck," *First Things* 48 (December, 1994): 44-50.

Welsh, Anne-Marie. "Twice Blessed," *Faith* (May/June 2006): 12-15.

Wright, John. "Pope John XXIII Revisited: What Was the Real Mind of Pope John?," *Homiletic & Pastoral Review* 73 (November, 1972): 10-24.

Wuerl, Donald. "Retired Bishop of Greensburg, Holy Priest of Pittsburgh," *The Pittsburgh Catholic* (16 June, 1995): 1.

Abbreviations

AAS ....Acta Apostolicae Sedis
ABR...The American Benedictine Review
ACQR ....The American Catholic Quarterly Review
AHR..American Historical Review
ASVA.................................Archives of Saint Vincent Archabbey
CBQ.. The Catholic Biblical Quarterly
CHR.. The Catholic Historical Review
DAB............................The Dictionary of American Biography
WPHM.....The Western Pennsylvania Historical Magazine

NOTES

[1]Paul Delatte, *The Rule of Saint Benedict: A Commentary*, trans. by Justin McCann (Latrobe, PA: The Archabbey Press, 1959), 81-82. For this edition of Delatte's commentary and Saint Vincent, see Jerome Oetgen, *Mission to America: A History of Saint Vincent Archabbey, the First Benedictine Monastery in the United States* (Washington, D. C.: The Catholic University of America Press, 2000), 312.

[2]Gregory the Great, *Dialogues* II. 28-29: Adalbert de Vogüé, ed., *Gregory the Great: The Life of Saint Benedict*, trans. by Hilary Costello and Eoin de Bhaldraithe (Petersham, MA: St. Bede's Publications, 1993), 131-133; cf. Glenn W. Olsen, "The Benedictine Way of Life: Yesterday, Today, Tomorrow," *Communio* 11 (Spring, 1984): 41.

[3]Regis Canevin, *The Church Year: Its Seasons, Feasts, Fasts, Devotions, and Other Observances* (Union City, NJ: The Sign Press, 1928), 58.

[4]Tacitus, *Germania* 19: *plusque ibi boni mores valent quam alibi bonae leges*. See Theodor Mommsen, *The Provinces of the Roman Empire from Caesar to Diocletian*, vol. 1, trans. by William P. Dickson (London: Macmillan, 1909), 169; cf. Ronald Syme, *Tacitus*, vol. 1 (Oxford: Clarendon Press, 1958), 126.

[5]Benedicta Ward, *The Venerable Bede.* (Kalamazoo: Cistercian Publication, 1998), 136-137. For Bede's advice to Egbert, see Scott DeGregorio, "Bede's *In Ezram et Neemiam* and the Reform of the Northumbrian Church," *Speculum* 79 (January, 2004): 6-9.

[6]The foremost biography of Wimmer is by Jerome Oetgen, *An American Abbot: Boniface Wimmer, O. S. B., 1809-1887* (Washington, D. C.: The Catholic University of America Press, 1997). That of Oswald Moosmüller, *Bonifaz Wimmer, Erzabt von St. Vincent in Pennsylvanien* (New York: Benziger, 1891), has not been translated from the German; that of Felix Fellner, *Abbot Boniface and His*

Monks (1956), was privately printed and distributed. Dated but notable is Colman J. Barry, "Boniface Wimmer, Pioneer of the American Benedictines," *CHR* 41 (October, 1955): 272-296; cf. Joel Rippinger, *The Benedictine Order in the United States: An Interpretive History* (Collegeville: The Liturgical Press, 1990), 19-31.

[7]Paulinus Selle, "Building Constructions at St. Vincent," (B. A. Thesis, Saint Vincent College, 1936), 5; Omer U. Kline, *The Sportsmans Hall Parish, Later Named St. Vincent, 1790-1846* (Latrobe, PA: Archabbey Press, 1990), 5-7; Daniel J. Heisey, "The Estate of Peter Helbron," *Cumberland County History* 21 (Summer, 2004): 23-33.

[8]Rene Kollar, "Plans for an 18th-Century Benedictine Settlement in Western Pennsylvania: Bishop John Carroll and the English Benedictine Congregation," *Word and Spirit* 14 (1992): 3-11.; reprinted in Rene Kollar, *A Universal Appeal: Aspects of the Revival of Monasticism in the West in the 19th and Early 20th Centuries* (San Francisco: International Scholars Publications, 1996), 287-295. It will be remembered that the Jesuits had been missionaries in the northern United States and southern Canada, but in 1773 Pope Pius VI had suppressed them. In the 1790s Franciscan missionaries from Spain were still active in Mexico and California, but it seems Carroll wanted religious who were culturally akin to the majority of his flock. In addition, Carroll had been ordained in England by a Benedictine monk, Bishop Charles Walmesley.

[9]Here and what follows John Carroll to Michael Pembridge, 19 September, 1794, in Thomas O'Brien Hanley, ed., *The John Carroll Papers*, 2 (Notre Dame: University of Notre Dame Press, 1976), 129.

[10]John Henry Newman, "Rise and Progress of Universities," *Historical Sketches* 3 (London: Longmans, Green and Co., 1913), 128; see Daniel J. Heisey, "Cardinal Newman and Benedictine Education," *Newman Studies Journal* 1 (Fall, 2004): 43-44.

[11]Quoted in Jerome Oetgen, *An American Abbot*, 63.

[12]Maxine Benson, ed., *From Pittsburgh to the Rocky Mountains: Major Stephen Long's Expedition, 1819-1820* (Golden, CO: Fulcrum, Inc., 1988), 13.

[13]Ibid.

[14]Ibid., 13-14.

[15]Ibid., 15. For a twentieth-century view of the same terrain, see: Brian A. Butko, *Pennsylvania Traveler's Guide: The Lincoln Highway* (Mechanicsburg, PA: Stackpole Books, 1996), 235-239.

[16]Quoted in Jerome Oetgen, *An American Abbot*, 140.

[17]Hubert Van Zeller, *The Benedictine Idea* (London: Burns & Oates, 1959), 200.

[18]Felix Fellner, "Boniface Wimmer," DAB, 371.

[19]Anselm Anthony Ober, "An Historical Sketch of the Establishment and Development of St. Vincent Seminary," (B. A. thesis, Saint Vincent College, 1938), 52. For Ober's obituary, see "Fr. Anselm A. Ober, O. S. B.," *Saint Vincent* 34 (Fall, 2000): 27.

[20]Ober, "Historical Sketch," 52.

[21]Ibid.

[22]On the flyleaf of the first volume someone penciled, *Hic textus est, cui studuit Revmus Abbas noster* (Bonif. Wimer); "This is the text from which our Reverend Abbot (Boniface Wimmer) studied."

[23]Ober, "Historical Sketch," 56; cf. Felix Fellner, "Archabbot Boniface Wimmer as an Educator," *The National Benedictine Educational Association Bulletin* 25 (December, 1942): 10-11.

[24]Callistus Edie, "Demetrius di Marogna," *The Scriptorium* 9 (Easter, 1949): 7-10; Oetgen, *Mission to America*, 87, 106-107.

[25]John Tracy Ellis, "A Short History of Seminary Education: II—Trent to Today," in James Michael Lee and Louis J. Putz, eds., *Seminary Education in a Time of Change* (Notre Dame: Fides Publishers, 1965), 31; John Tracy Ellis, "From Trent to the 1960's," *Essays in Seminary Education* (Notre Dame: Fides Publishers, 1967), 42.

[26]*Annus Mariano-Benedictinus, sive Sancti Illustres Ordinis Bendicti* (Salzburg: J. B. Mayr, 1668).

[27]Paul Roger Taylor, "Boniface Wimmer and Saint Vincent College: The Beginning of American Benedictine Education," (Ph. D. dissertation, Boston College, 1998), 21.

[28]Ober, "Historical Sketch," 52; cf. Jerome Oetgen, *An American Abbot*, 80; Oetgen, *Mission to America*, 64-65, 69; Brian D. Boosel, "Boniface Wimmer, O.S.B., and the Foundation of Saint Vincent Seminary," (M. A. Thesis, Slippery Rock University, 2004), 88-91. I have supplemented these accounts with the recollections of Brother Patrick Lacey, O. S. B., who reports that in 1949, when he entered the monastic community at Saint Vincent, the lay brothers were still reciting the thrice-daily Rosary in German.

[29]Quoted in Jerome Oetgen, *Mission to America*, 103.

³⁰For an English translation, see Jerome Oetgen, *Mission to America*, 513-515.

³¹Aloysius Plaisance, "Emmeran Bliemel, O. S. B., Heroic Confederate Chaplain," *ABR* 17 (June, 1966): 209-216; Peter J. Meaney, "Valiant Chaplain of the Bloody Tenth," *Tennessee Historical Quarterly* 41 (Spring, 1982): 37-47; Jerome Oetgen, *An American Abbot*, 252; Oetgen, *Mission to America*, 121.

³²"Right Rev. Boniface Krug, O. S. B., Archabbot of Monte Cassino, Italy," *St. Vincent College Journal* 19 (October, 1909): 1-8; Oetgen, *Mission to America*, 89-90.

³³Sabatino Iannetta, *Henry W. Longfellow and Montecassino* (Boston: B. Humphries, 1940), 30-31; 81-82.

³⁴"Monte Cassino," *Longfellow: Poetical Works* (New York: Oxford University Press, 1979), 329.

³⁵Quoted in Iannetta, *Henry W. Longfellow and Montecassino*, 37.

³⁶"Rt. Rev. Boniface Krug," *St. Vincent College Journal* 19 (October, 1909): 3.

³⁷Raymond H. Schmandt, "The Friendship Between Bishop Regis Canevin of Pittsburgh and Dr. Lawrence Flick of Philadelphia," *WPHM* 61 (October, 1978): 284.

³⁸Raymond H. Schmandt, "The Friendship Between Bishop Regis Canevin of Pittsburgh and Dr. Lawrence Flick of Philadelphia," *WPHM* 61 (October, 1978): 290; Canevin's emphasis.

³⁹*Catholic Pittsburgh's One Hundred Years* (Chicago: Loyola University Press, 1943), 68.

⁴⁰Ibid., 71.

⁴¹Ibid., 86.

⁴²Ibid., 68.

⁴³"Address by the Rt. Rev. Bishop," *St. Vincent College Journal* 30 (December, 1920): 89.

⁴⁴Ibid.

⁴⁵Ibid.

⁴⁶Ibid., 90.

⁴⁷Ibid.

⁴⁸"Resignation of Bishop Canevin," *St. Vincent College Journal* 30 (January, 1921): 114.

⁴⁹Ibid. See also, "The Episcopal Change," *The Seminarists' Symposium* 3 (1920-1921): 116: "He was truly an *alter Christus*, because he gave his life for his sheep."

[50]James Hennesey, *The First Council of the Vatican: The American Experience* (New York: Herder and Herder, 1963), 36-37.

[51]Ibid., 72-73.

[52]Walter Bagehot, "The Political Aspect of the Oecumenical Council," in Norman St. John Stevas, ed., *The Collected Works of Walter Bagehot* 8 (London: The Economist, 1974): 169. Bagehot's essay first appeared in *The Economist* (11 December, 1869).

[53]Ibid.

[54]Ibid.

[55]Charles Hodge, "Letter to Pope Pius IX," *The Banner of Truth* (April, 1998): 25. This letter, its manuscript in the Princeton Seminary archives, had remained unpublished for nearly 130 years.

[56]Boniface Wimmer, Preface to Joseph Pennacchi, *De Honorii I Romani Pontificis Causa in Concilio VI* (Regensburg: F. Pustet, 1870); see James Hennesey, *The First Council of the Vatican*, 230; cf. Jerome Oetgen, *An American Abbot*, 310-311.

[57]Norman P. Tanner, ed., *Decrees of the Ecumenical Councils*, vol. 2 (Washington, D. C.: Georgetown University Press, 1990), 808. Tanner gives both the Latin text and English translation, used here.

[58]Ibid., 809; see John Paul II, Encyclical Letter, *Fides et Ratio* (1998), 53.

[59]*Acta et Decreta Concilii Plenarii Baltimorensis Tertii* (Baltimore: John Murphy, 1886), 85-89; cf. Oetgen, Mission to America, 198-199.

[60]George William Mundelein, *Two Crowded Years* (Chicago: Extension Press, 1918), 107. For Mundelein at Saint Vincent, see "The Rt. Rev. George W. Mundelein, D. D., '92," *St. Vincent College Journal* 19 (October, 1909): 38-40; Gerard Bridge, "The Rt. Rev. George Mundelein, D. D.: Archbishop-Elect of Chicago," *St. Vincent College Journal* 25 (January, 1915): 236-239; Edrward R. Kantowicz, *Corporation Sole: Cardinal Mundelein and Chicago Catholicism* (Notre Dame: University of Notre Dame Press, 1983), 5.

[61]For example, neither Monsignor Ellis, American Catholicism, nor Jay P. Dolan, *The American Catholic Experience: A History from Colonial Times to the Present* (Garden City, NY: Doubleday, 1985), refer to Wimmer or Saint Vincent. Father James Hennesey, a Jesuit, in *American Catholics: A History of the Roman Catholic Community in the United States* (New York: Oxford University Press, 1981), 81, refers to "Benedictines from Bavaria" in 1846 occupying Sportsman's Hall.

[62]See Jerome Oetgen, *An American Abbot*, 112.

[63]Quoted in Oetgen, *An American Abbot*, 300. Martin Marty (1834-1896) was a monk of the Benedictine abbey of Einsiedeln, Switzerland; in 1860 he was sent to Indiana to rescue Einsiedeln's faltering priory, now known as Saint Meinrad Archabbey. In 1880 Pope Leo XIII made Marty bishop of the Dakota Territory. See Joel Rippinger, *The Benedictine Order in the United States*, 49-54.

[64]Frederick Jackson Turner, "The Significance of the Frontier in American History," *The Frontier in American History* (New York: Holt, Rhinehart, and Winston, 1920), 3.

[65]Pius X, Apostolic Constitution, *Sapienti consilio* 6.2, AAS 1 (1909) 12; see John Tracy Ellis, *American Catholicism* 2nd ed. (Chicago: University of Chicago Press, 1969), 124.

[66]Paul Roger Taylor, "Boniface Wimmer and Saint Vincent College: The Beginnings of American Benedictine Education" (Ph. D. dissertation, Boston College, 1998), 20.

[67]For what follows, see: Daniel J. Heisey, "The Works of Henry Ganss," *Cumberland County History* 21 (Summer, 2004): 13-22.

[68]James F. Loughlin, "The Higher and Lower Education of the American Priesthood," *ACQR* 15 (January, 1890): 108.

[69]For this anecdote, see [H. G. Ganss] "Fugitive Recollections, Musical and Unmusical, 1868-1878, by an Old Alumnus," 50. Typescript, ASVA.

[70]Ibid., 38.

[71]See "Notes and Comments," *CHR* 49 (April, 1963): 147.

[72]Felix Fellner, "The 'Two Cities' of Otto of Freising and Its Influence on the Catholic Philosophy of History," *CHR* 20 (July, 1934): 154. Fellner had given this paper in December, 1933, at the fourteenth annual meeting of the American Catholic Historical Association, of which in 1925 Fellner had served as vice president.

[73]Ibid.

[74]Ibid., 160.

[75]Francis A. Glenn, *Shepherds of the Faith: 1843-1993: A Brief History of the Bishops of the Catholic Diocese of Pittsburgh*. (Pittsburgh: Catholic Diocese of Pittsburgh, 1993), 143.

[76]David G. McCullough, *The Johnstown Flood* (New York: Simon & Schuster, 1968), 177.

[77]Philip Jenkins, *The New Anti-Catholicism: The Last Acceptable Prejudice* (New York: Oxford University Press, 2003), 30; cf. Ellis, *American Catholicism*,

124-125.

[78]R. W. Southern, *Western Society and the Church in the Middle Ages* (New York: Penguin Books, 1970), 80.

[79]Ibid.

[80]Anton C. Pegis, *The Middle Ages and Philosophy: Some Reflections on the Ambivalnce of Modern Scholasticism* (Chicago: Henry Regnery Co., 1963), 73.

[81]Jerome Oetgen, *Mission to America*, 260.

[82]For what follows, see Ober, "Historical Sketch," 32-39; cf. Oetgen, *Mission to America*, 260-262.

[83]"The Rev. Vitus Kratzer, O. S. B.," *St. Vincent College Journal* 26 (December, 1916): 183-188; "The Rev Vitus Kratzer, O. S. B., J. C. D., D. D.," *The Seminarists' Symposium* 1 (1918-1919): 81; Jerome Oetgen, *Mission to America*, 261-262.

[84]"The Rev. Vitus Kratzer, O. S. B.," *St. Vincent College Journal* 26 (December, 1916): 186.

[85]Ober, "Historical Sketch," 25; cf. Oetgen, *Mission to America*, 271-272.

[86]Joel Rippinger, *The Benedictine Order in the United States*, 159.

[87]Philip Jenkins, "The Ku Klux Klan in Pennsylvania, 1920-1940," *WPHM* 69 (April, 1986): 128-129; cf. Philip Jenkins, *Hoods and Shirts: The Extreme Right in Pennsylvania, 1925-1950* (Chapel Hill: The University of North Carolina Press, 1997), 67.

[88]Ober, "Historical Sketch," 18.

[89]Francis X. Reuss, "Leaves from the Diary of Francis X. Reuss, '67-'69," *St. Vincent College Journal* 18 (June, 1909): 439. Reuss (1847-1913) was librarian of Philadelphia's American Catholic Historical Society and in 1898 published *Biographical Cyclopedia of the Catholic Hierarchy of the United States*, 1784-1898.

[90]Ober, "Historical Sketch," 18; cf. Selle, "Building Construction at St. Vincent," 37; Oetgen, *Mission to America*, 267.

[91]Ibid.

[92]Anselm Ober, "Historical Sketch," 20.

[93]Paulinus Selle, "Building Constructions at St. Vincent," 70.

[94]Anselm Ober, "Historical Sketch," 21.

[95]Selle, "Building Constructions at St. Vincent," 71.

[96]Ibid., 72.

[97]Charles Owen Rice, "Latrobe Seminary 'Tough and Tolerant'," *The Pittsburgh Catholic* (17 April, 1992): 5; reprinted in Charles J. McCollester, ed., *Fighter with a Heart: Writings of Charles Owen Rice, Pittsburgh Labor Priest* (Pittsburgh:

University of Pittsburgh Press, 1996), 19; see "Msgr. Charles Owen Rice Honored," *Leaven* 13 (Fall, 2004): 32. Begun in 1988, *Leaven* is the newsletter of Saint Vincent Seminary. See also, John Franko, "Champion of Justice," *The Pittsburgh Catholic* (25 November, 2005): 12.

[98]Rice, "Latrobe Seminary 'Tough and Tolerant'," *The Pittsburgh Catholic* (17 April, 1992): 5; McCollester, ed., *Fighter with a Heart*, 20.

[99]Ibid.

[100]Anselm Ober, "Historical Sketch," 53-54.

[101]Patrick J. McGeever, *Rev. Charles Owen Rice: Apostle of Contradiction* (Pittsburgh: Duquesne University Press, 1989), 41; Kenneth J. Heineman, *A Catholic New Deal: Religion and Reform in Depression Pittsburgh* (University Park: Pennsylvania State University Press, 1999), 15.

[102]"Catholics & Chance," *Time* (27 December, 1937): 24.

[103]Charles Owen Rice, "America's Darkest Decade," in McCollester, ed., *Fighter with a Heart*, 27; cf. Rice, "Remembering Fr. James R. Cox," *The Pittsburgh Catholic* (15 December, 1989): 5; reprinted in McCollester, ed., *Fighter with a Heart*, 20: "Fr. Cox was a reform Republican."

[104]Thomas H. Coode and John D. Petrarulo, "The Odyssey of Pittsburgh's Father Cox," *WPHM* 55 (July, 1971): 233.

[105]See Oswald von Nell-Breuning, *Reorganization of Social Economy*, trans. by Bernard W. Dempsey (Milwaukee: The Bruce Publishing Co., 1936), 305-307; Wilhelm Röpke, *A Humane Economy: The Social Framework of the Free Market*, trans. by Elizabeth Henderson (Chicago: Henry Regnery Co., 1960), 13; John Paul II, Encyclical Letter, *Centesimus Annus* (1991), 47-49; Avery Dulles, "*Centesimus Annus* and the Renewal of Culture," *Journal of Markets & Morality* 2 (Spring, 1999): 2-3.

[106]Charles Owen Rice, "Remembering Fr. James R. Cox," *The Pittsburgh Catholic* (15 December, 1989): 5; McCollester, ed., *Fighter with a Heart*, 21.

[107]Rice, "Remembering Fr. James R. Cox," *The Pittsburgh Catholic* (15 December, 1989): 5; McCollester, *Fighter with a Heart*, 20.

[108]James R. Cox, *Illustrated Lectures: 15 Minute Sermons Cut to One Minute.* (Pittsburgh: The Catholic Observer, n. d.). Most of the cartoons have no date, but some are dated 1930.

[109]Pius Engelbert, *Geschichte des Benediktinerkollegs St. Anselm in Rom.* (Rome: Sant' Anselmo, 1988), 149-154.

[110]"Priests Members in Bible Society," *Saint Vincent Journal* 48 (15 February,

1939): 3; Charles H. Pickar, "Biblical News," *CBQ* 1 (July, 1939): 267-271.

[111]Clifford Stevens, "The Saga of Conception Abbey," *Homiletic & Pastoral Review* 73 (January, 1973): 44. For Cummins, see: Mary Faith Schuster, "Father Patrick Cummins (1880-1968)," *ABR* 19 (March, 1968): 112-115; "Father Patrick Cummins, O. S. B.," *CBQ* 30 (April, 1968): 240-241.

[112]Patrick Cummins, "Rev. Justin Krellner, O. S. B.: In Memoriam," *CBQ* 12 (January, 1950): 90.

[113]"Archabbey's Scripture Scholar Called Suddenly by Death," *The St. Vincent Journal* 59 (September, 1949): 2.

[114]Rembert Weakland, "Personal Memories," in Gerardo J. Bekes, ed., *Sant' Anselmo: Saggi Storici e di Attualità.* (Rome: Sant' Anselmo, 1988), 285.

[115]Hubert A. Macko, *Grammar of the Slovak Language* (Scranton: Obrana, 1926); see Rene Kollar, *Saint Vincent Archabbey and Its Role in the Development of Slovak-American Culture and History* (Latrobe, PA: Archabbey Publications, 1996), 4.

[116]Oetgen, *Mission to America*, 428.

[117]Gerald B. Phelan, "The Pontifical Institute of Mediaeval Studies at Toronto." *The Dublin Review* 481 (Autumn, 1959): 230.

[118]Ibid., 231. For Phelan's career, see Anton Pegis, "Gerald Bernard Phelan," *Mediaeval Studies* 27 (1966): i-v. In 1949 Phelan (1892-1965) came to Saint Vincent and delivered the third annual Wimmer Lecture, published in 1960 by the Archabbey Press as *The Wisdom of Saint Anselm*.

[119]Jerome Oetgen, *Mission to America*, 310.

[120]John XXIII, Apostolic Constitution, *Veterum Sapientiae, AAS* 54 (1962): 130.

[121]John Wright, "Pope John XXIII Revisited: What Was the Real Mind of Pope John?," *Homiletic & Pastoral Review* 73 (November, 1972): 20; reprinted in R. Stephen Almagno, ed., *Resonare Christum: A Selection from the Sermons, Addresses, Interviews, and Papers of Cardinal John J. Wright*, vol. 3 (San Francisco: Ignatius Press, 1995), 291.

[122]Christopher Dawson, "American Education and Christian Culture," *ABR* 9 (Spring/Summer, 1958): 8.

[123]Ibid., 8.

[124]Ibid., 15; Dawson's emphasis. Cf. Christopher Dawson, *The Crisis of Western Education* (New York: Sheed and Ward, 1961), 97-99;133-134; Glenn W. Olsen, "American Culture and Liberal Ideology in the Thought of Christopher

Dawson," *Communio* 22 (Fall, 1995): 718. In 1959 Dawson (1889-1970) came to Saint Vincent and delivered the annual Wimmer Lecture, his topic being "The Movement Towards Christian Unity in the Nineteenth Century."

[125]See George Weigel, "Re-Viewing Vatican II: An Interview with George A. Lindbeck," *First Things* 48 (December, 1994): 44-50.

[126]*Optatam totius*, AAS 58 (1966): 713; Norman P. Tanner, ed., *Decrees of the Ecumenical Councils*, vol. 2, 947: *Optatam totius ecclesiae renovationem*; my translation; cf. Walter M. Abbott, ed., *The Documents of Vatican II* (New York: Herder and Herder, 1966), 437, "wished-for renewal of the whole Church;" Austin Flannery, ed., *Vatican Council II*, vol. 1 (Northport, NY: Costello Publishing Co., 1996), 707, "the desired renewal of the whole Church."

[127]Jerome Oetgen, *Mission to America*, 434-435.

[128]Demetrius Dumm, *Cherish Christ Above All: The Bible in the Rule of Benedict* (New York: Paulist Press, 1996), 119.

[129]Jerome Oetgen, *Mission to America*, 435.

[130]For this address, see Anselm M. Albareda, "Origins of Benedictine Schools, Scriptoria, and Libraries," *The Catholic Library World* 29 (May-June, 1958): 447-450. Albareda's tedious delivery is preserved in oral tradition. For Albareda himself, see "Cardinal Albareda," *The Tablet* (30 July, 1966): 879-880.

[131]Jerome Oetgen, *Mission to America*, 466-478.

[132]"Into the Mystic with John," *U. S. Catholic* 68 (April, 2003): 17.

[133]Ibid.

[134]Ibid.

[135]For a complete list of rectors, see Appendix 1.

[136]*50 Years on the Journey: Diocese of Greensburg*, 1951-2001. Supplement to *The Catholic Accent* (8 March, 2001): 12.

[137]Ibid., 13; cf. "Bishop William Connare of Greensburg, a Pittsburgh Priest," *The Pittsburgh Catholic* (16 June, 1995): 12.

[138]"Synodal Sermon," *First Synod of the Diocese of Greensburg* (Greensburg: Diocese of Greensburg, 1963) 136.

[139]"Decree of Prayer," *First Synod of the Diocese of Greensburg*, 131.

[140]Vincent A. Yzermans, ed., *American Participation in the Second Vatican Council* (New York: Sheed and Ward, 1967), 162.

[141]*50 Years on the Journey*, 13.

[142]Michael Novak, *The Open Church: Vatican II, Act II* (New York: Macmillan Co., 1964), 329.

[143]Donald Wuerl, "Retired Bishop of Greensburg, Holy Priest of Pittsburgh," *The Pittsburgh Catholic* (16 June, 1995): 1.

[144]"Father Paulinus Retires After 57 Consecutive Years Teaching," *Leaven* 7 (Fall, 1997): 1.

[145]Jerome Oetgen, *Mission to America*, 367, 379.

[146]"Father Paulinus Retires After 57 Consecutive Years Teaching," *Leaven* 7 (Fall, 1997): 16.

[147]Ibid.

[148]Ibid.

[149]"Father Paulinus Celebrates 50 Years of Teaching," *Leaven* 1 (Spring, 1989): 1. Another but smaller gathering marked his ninetieth birthday: "Professor Emeritus Celebrates 90th," *Leaven* (Spring, 2004): 16.

[150]Claude J. Peifer, "The Formation of Non-Clerical Junior Monks," *ABR* 33 (March, 1982): 36.

[151]Ibid., 45.

[152]Ibid., 36.

[153]See Fulton J. Sheen, *The Priest Is Not His Own* (New York: McGraw-Hill Book Co., 1963).

[154]"Pontifical Degree Status Attained," *Leaven* 9 (Winter, 2000): 1, 4.

[155]"Hispanic Ministries Program Expanding," *Leaven* 9 (Summer/Fall, 2000): 4-5.

[156]R. Todd Erkel, "How John Marous Sets the Pace," *Pitt Magazine* (December, 1989): 21.

[157]Gregory L. Miles, "How Westinghouse Is Revving Up After the Rebound," *Business Week* (28 March, 1988): 46.

[158]R. Todd Erkel, "How John Marous Sets the Pace," *Pitt Magazine* (December, 1989): 22.

[159]John C. Marous, Jr., "Focus on Pastoral Stewardship," *Leaven* 11 (Spring, 2002): n. p. This essay is part of the Seminary's Annual Report, printed as part of this issue of *Leaven*.

[160]"Rabbi Presents Ancient Missal at Academic Dinner," *The Saint Vincent Journal* 56 (September, 1946): 26. Rabbi Freehof (1892-1990) was a biblical scholar and literary critic; see Barry Paris, "Reflections on a Lifetime Steeped in Books," *The Pittsburgh Post-Gazette* (13 December, 1982): 25, 30.

[161]Solomon B. Freehof, "The Bond of Worship," in Philip Scharper, ed., *Torah and Gospel: Jewish and Catholic Theology in Dialogue* (New York: Sheed and

Ward, 1966), 37-46.

[162]See Jason Z. Edelstein, "The Saint Vincent Touch," in Campion P. Gavaler, ed., *Saint Vincent: A Benedictine Place* (Latrobe, PA: Saint Vincent Archabbey, 1995), 35.

[163]See Richard David Wissolik, et al., eds, *Listen to Our Words: Oral Histories of the Jewish Community of Westmoreland County, Pennsylvania* (Latrobe, PA: Saint Vincent College, 1997), 19-30; "Seminary Guest Speakers," *Leaven* 11 (Spring, 2002): 26.

[164]William Stubbs, ed., *Keeping the Day: Contemplations of the Book of Exodus: A Festschrift Honoring Reverend Robert Vogelsang, D. D., 1926-1982* (Allison Park, PA: Pickwick Publications, 1985).

[165]Fred M. Rogers, "The Final Word Is Love," in Campion P. Gavaler, ed., *Saint Vincent: A Benedictine Place* (Latrobe, PA: Saint Vincent Archabbey, 1995) :25; reprinted in *Heart to Heart* 14 (Summer, 2003): 1. *Heart to Heart* is the newsletter of Saint Vincent Archabbey.

[166]Amy Hollingsworth, *The Simple Faith of Mister Rogers: Spiritual Insights from the World's Most Beloved Neighbor* (Nashville: Integrity Publishers, 2005), 78-79; cf. Daniel McGinn, "Everybody's Next-door Neighbor," *Newsweek* (10 March, 2003): 61.

[167]"Sesquicentennial Opens," *The Benedictine Monks of Saint Vincent Archabbey Monastery Newsletter* 8 (Spring/Summer, 1995): 1-2.

[168]"Elizabeth J. Roderick Center, Chapel of Saint Gregory the Great Dedicated," *Leaven* 7 (Fall, 1997): 1, 5, 9.

[169]Ibid., 5.

[170]Eden Simmons, "America's Top Seminaries," *Crisis* (October, 1997): 34.

[171]Kurt Belsole, "A Sense of Gratitude and Accomplishment," *Leaven* 12 (Spring, 2004): 4; "Extensive Renovation and Addition of Seminary Classroom Building Completed Through the Generosity of Mrs. Annette Brownfield," *Leaven* 13 (Fall, 2004): 4-7; cf. Theresa Schwab, "Why We Give," *Quarterly* 2 (Spring, 2004); 8. To this information I add my own observations.

[172]"Pro-Life Activities Intensify," *Leaven* 2 (Spring, 1990): 1. Nearly each successive Spring issue of *Leaven* features the Seminary's participation in the March for Life.

[173]Angelo Scola, *Test Everything, Hold Fast to What Is Good: An Interview with Hans Urs von Balthasar* (San Francisco: Ignatius Press, 1989), 92.

[174]Ibid., 93.

[175]Ibid. In 2003, Pope John Paul II made Angelo Scola Cardinal Patriarch of Venice, Italy.

[176]Thomas Acklin, "Tomorrow's Priests," *The Priest* 54 (December, 1998): 42. Acklin responds to Albert DiIanni, "A View of Religious Vocations," *America* (28 February, 1998): 8-12. Acklin has developed the theme of this article in his book, *The Unchanging Heart of the Priesthood: A Faith Perspective on the Mystery and Reality of Priesthood in the Church* (Steubenville, OH: Emmaus Road Publishing, 2005). For a profile of seminarians with ties to Saint Vincent, see Anne-Marie Welsh, "Twice Blessed," *Faith* (May/June 2006): 12-15; see also Betsy Benson, "Men in Black," *Pittsburgh* (April, 2004): 64-83; cf. Christine Stark Purcell, "My Son the Monk," *St. Anthony Messenger* 110 (June, 2002): 12-16.

[177]Acklin, "Tomorrow's Priests," *The Priest* 54 (December, 1998): 43.

[178]Kurt Belsole, "Stewards of the Mysteries: Training Seminarians for Liturgical Leadership," *Antiphon* 8 (2003): 26.

[179]This date Americans will, of course, recognize as the 230th anniversary of "the midnight ride of Paul Revere," immortalized by Longfellow's poem.

[180]Emily Stimpson, "Tomorrow's Priests Will Be 'Good Fruit,' Rector Says," *Our Sunday Visitor* (7 May, 2006):   ; see also, Kurt Belsole, "Fatherhood from the Heart of the Church," *National Catholic Register* (18-24 June, 2006): 9.

[181]Scott Hahn, "Scripture and Liturgy: Inseparably United," *Origins* 35 (16 March, 2006): 648-653; see Kim Metzgar, "Inaugural Lecture of the Pope Benedict XVI Chair of Biblical Theolgy and Liturgical Proclamation Given by Dr. Scott Hahn," *Leaven* 14 (Spring, 2006): 2-4.

[182]Scott Hahn and Kimberly Hahn, *Rome Sweet Home: Our Journey to Catholicism* (San Francisco: Ignatius Press, 1993). Catholic reviewers compared this book with Thomas Merton's conversion memoir, *The Seven Storey Mountain* (1948): Matthew V. Reilley, "Finding Their Way Home," *Homiletic & Pastoral Review* 94 (June, 1994): 74-76.

[183]"Commencement Address on John Paul II's Papacy," *Leaven* 9 (Summer/Fall, 2000): 17. Weigel had high marks also for Saint Vincent College: George Weigel, "Catholicism's Bright Future: Seven Signs in America that the End is Nowhere Near," *This Rock* 14 (September, 2003): 16. Cf. Joseph Ratzinger, *God and the World: Believing and Living in Our Time, a Conversation with Peter Seewald*, trans. by Henry Taylor. (San Francisco: Ignatius Press, 2002), 447: Young seminarians, priests, and religious today live in "a great joy in their faith, also particularly intending to read again the Fathers and Thomas Aquinas."